The O.J. Simpson Trial

by Earle Rice Jr.

Lucent Books, San Diego, CA

Other books in the Famous Trials series:

The Dred Scott Decision
The Nuremberg Trials
The Salem Witch Trials
The Scopes Trial
The Trial of Socrates

Library of Congress Cataloging-in-Publication Data
Rice, Earle.
    The O.J. Simpson trial / by Earle Rice, Jr.
        p. cm. — (Famous trials)
    Includes bibliographical references and index.
    Summary: An overview of the noted O.J. Simpson murder trial and the events preceding it.
    ISBN 1-56006-271-1 (alk. paper)
    1. Simpson, O.J., 1947–   —Trials, litigation, etc.—Juvenile literature. 2. Trials (Murder)—California—Los Angeles—Juvenile literature. [1. Simpson, O.J., 1947–   —Trials, litigation, etc. 2. Trials (Murder)] I. Title. II. Series: Famous trials series.
KF224.S485R53   1997
345.73'02623'0979494—dc20
[347.3052523'0979494]   96-34420
                                                                   CIP
                                                                    AC

Copyright © 1997 by Lucent Books, Inc.
P.O. Box 289011
San Diego, CA 92198-9011
Printed in the U.S.A.

Table of Contents

Foreword

"The law is not an end in and of itself, nor does it provide ends. It is preeminently a means to serve what we think is right."

William J. Brennan Jr.

THE CONCEPT OF JUSTICE AND THE RULE OF LAW are hallmarks of Western civilization, manifested perhaps most visibly in widely famous and dramatic court trials. These trials include such important and memorable personages as the ancient Greek philosopher Socrates, who was accused and convicted of corrupting the minds of his society's youth in 399 B.C.; the French maiden and military leader Joan of Arc, accused and convicted of heresy against the church in 1431; to former football star O.J. Simpson, acquitted of double murder in 1995. These and other well-known and controversial trials constitute the most public, and therefore most familiar, demonstrations of a Western legal tradition that dates back through the ages. Although no one is certain when the first law code appeared or when the first formal court trials were held, Babylonian ruler Hammurabi introduced the first known law code in about 1760 B.C. It remains unclear how this code was administered, and no records of specific trials have survived. What is clear, however, is that humans have always sought to govern behavior and define actions in terms of law.

Almost all societies have made laws and prosecuted people for going against those laws, but the question of which behaviors to sanction and which to censure has always been controversial and remains in flux. Some, such as Roman orator and legislator Cicero, argue that laws are simply applications of universal standards. Cicero believed that humanity would agree on what constituted illegal behavior and that human laws were a mere extension of natural laws. "True law is right reason in agreement with nature," he wrote,

5

world-wide in scope, unchanging, everlasting. . . . We may not oppose or alter that law, we cannot abolish it, we cannot be freed from its obligations by any legislature. . . . This [natural] law does not differ for Rome and for Athens, for the present and for the future. . . . It is and will be valid for all nations and all times.

Cicero's rather optimistic view has been contradicted throughout history, however. For every law made to preserve harmony and set universal standards of behavior, another has been born of fear, prejudice, greed, desire for power, and a host of other motives. History is replete with individuals defying and fighting to change such laws—and even to topple governments that dictate such laws. Abolitionists fought against slavery, civil rights leaders fought for equal rights, millions throughout the world have fought for independence—these constitute a minimum of reasons for which people have sought to overturn laws that they believed to be wrong or unjust. In opposition to Cicero, then, many others, such as eighteenth-century English poet and philosopher William Godwin, believe humans must be constantly vigilant against bad laws. As Godwin said in 1793:

Laws we sometimes call the wisdom of our ancestors. But this is a strange imposition. It was as frequently the dictate of their passion, of timidity, jealousy, a monopolizing spirit, and a lust of power that knew no bounds. Are we not obliged perpetually to renew and remodel this misnamed wisdom of our ancestors? To correct it by a detection of their ignorance, and a censure of their intolerance?

Lucent Books' *Famous Trials* series showcases trials that exemplify both society's praiseworthy condemnation of universally unacceptable behavior, and its misguided persecution of individuals based on fear and ignorance, as well as trials that leave open the question of whether justice has been done. Each volume begins by setting the scene and providing a historical context to show how society's mores influence the trial process and the verdict. Each book goes on to present a detailed and lively account of the trial, including liberal use of primary source material such as direct testimony, lawyers' summations, and contemporary and modern commentary. In addition, sidebars throughout the text create a broader context by presenting illuminating details about important points of law, information on key personalities, and important distinctions related to civil, federal, and criminal procedures. Thus, all of the primary and secondary source material included in both the text and the sidebars demonstrates to readers the sources and methods historians use to derive information and conclusions about such events.

Lastly, each *Famous Trials* volume includes one or more of the following comprehensive tools that motivate readers to pursue further reading and research. A timeline allows readers to see the scope of the trial at a glance, annotated bibliographies provide both sources for further research and a thorough list of works consulted, a glossary helps students with unfamiliar words and concepts, and a comprehensive index permits quick scanning of the book as a whole.

The insight of Oliver Wendell Holmes Jr., distinguished Supreme Court justice, exemplifies the theme of the *Famous Trials* series. Taken from *The Common Law*, published in 1881, Holmes remarked: "The life of the law has not been logic, it has been experience." That "experience" consists mainly in how laws are applied in society and challenged in the courts, a process resulting in differing outcomes from one generation to the next. Thus, the *Famous Trials* series encourages readers to examine trials within a broader historical and social context.

Introduction

The Highs and the Lows of O.J. and Nicole

*I*N DECEMBER 1973 FOOTBALL FANS *around the nation sat with eyes glued to their television screens. A telecast of the game between the Buffalo Bills and the New York Jets from Shea Stadium had drawn the attention of millions of viewers on the promise of history about to be made. The Bills' banner running back needed only four more yards to break Jim Brown's ten-year-old National Football League single season rushing record of 1,863 yards.*

The premier Buffalo ballcarrier did not fail the 47,740 shivering fans who had braved the snow and wintry gusts in Flushing's stadium that afternoon. Late in the first quarter, the Buffalo ace slipped through the left side of the line and powered his way through the snow for six yards. Jim Brown's record fell.

The pumped-up crowd roared for more, and the Buffalo running back, adrenaline surging, obliged. Despite the treacherous footing of Shea's snow and ice, he ran for 140 total yards, setting the new rushing record for a single season at 2,003 yards and becoming the first player ever to rush over 2,000 yards in a season.

In the snow and slush, the new record holder had plunged across the line that separates football's immortals from those who only play the game. O.J. Simpson had arrived.

The Best of the Best

Orenthal James Simpson adapted quickly to the snow and freezing cold. Although San Francisco born and California bred, the two-time all-American running back from the University of Southern California zigged and zagged his way to fame and wealth on the frozen turf of Buffalo's War Memorial Stadium and Rich Stadium. To a youth who had played his entire college football career in the warmer, gentler environs of San Francisco and Los Angeles, the windswept, blue-collar city on the shores of Lake Erie might have understandably appeared less than inviting. But in 1969, when the Buffalo Bills, then of the American Football League, offered Simpson a contract rumored to be worth some $350,000, he grabbed the money and ran with it. And he didn't stop running for eleven more spectacular years.

Simpson began his climb to the pinnacle of football acclaim and financial security at City College in his hometown of San Francisco. While struggling to bring up his grade point average at CCSF, he turned in a record-setting performance on the football field, scoring fifty-four touchdowns in two seasons. College

While playing for the Buffalo Bills in New York, O.J. Simpson runs 140 yards to become the first player in football history to pass 2,000 yards in one season.

O.J. Simpson accepts the Heisman Trophy for outstanding football player for his performance at the University of Southern California.

football scouts from all over the country flocked to the Simpson door in Potrero Hill, an impoverished section of the city by the Golden Gate. But the young football sensation, soon to be known as "the Juice," had long since aimed at playing for USC. He dreamed of "that [Trojan] white horse. . . *gallopin'*" around the track of the Los Angeles Coliseum, next to the USC campus, each time he scored a touchdown.

In 1967 Simpson led the Trojans to a national collegiate title. The next year he won the Heisman Trophy—an annual award given to college football's outstanding player. As the best of the best collegiate players, Simpson's future in professional football was assured. O.J. was on his way.

Tribute to the Gods

Simpson has often credited his first wife, Marguerite Whitely, whom he married in a Catholic ceremony on June 24, 1967, for her major contribution to his early success. Marguerite's stabilizing influence in his life helped to turn him away from Potrero Hill's youth gangs and to keep him focused on athletics as a path out of the ghetto. Their union produced a daughter, Arnelle, in 1968, and a son, Jason, in 1970, further contributing to O.J.'s motivation. But their marriage was fated to fail in twelve years.

In 1969 O.J. graduated from the University of Southern California with a diploma in one hand and a scrapbook full of clippings of his phenomenal gridiron feats in the other. As the undisputed king of college football, O.J. looked forward to cashing in on his collegiate fame and singular athletic abilities. His enormous natural talent, coupled with a compulsive—some would say *obsessive*—need to work tirelessly at everything he did, soon brought even greater fame to Simpson as a pro football commodity.

From the earliest recollections of family and friends, Simpson was always busy, always driven to be *doing* something—a virtual workaholic. He never forgot that as a kid he had narrowly escaped a life of poverty and possibly of crime. O.J. had no intention of ever returning to one of the numberless Potrero Hills of the world. Hard work could and would set him free.

Once the big money started pouring into the Simpson coffers, O.J. was quick to realize that a career in professional football, even to those who avoid career-ending injuries, is either short or very short. From the day he first donned a Bills uniform, he seemed to understand better than most of his play-for-pay peers that the highs of a few Sunday afternoons in the sun give way all too soon to the lows of Monday morning obscurity. He started at once to prepare himself for life after football.

O.J. recognized his value as a salable commodity. So, while he went about toppling records on the playing fields of the American and National Football Leagues, he also marketed his all-American boyish charm and diverse capabilities to television, the movies, and commercial endorsements. Whether motivated by fear

Simpson with first wife Marguerite, who Simpson credited with keeping him stable and on track during his early football career.

of failing or insatiable ambition, O.J. established himself—almost simultaneously—as a football superstar, sports commentator, movie actor, and spokesperson for commercial products.

During O.J.'s early years with the Buffalo Bills, veteran sportscaster Howard Cosell, never gushing with compliments, deftly captured the essence of Buffalo's emerging sensation:

> Certainly O.J. has every skill a truly great running back needs. He's got the most spontaneous reflexes of anyone I've ever seen; he has an uncanny ability to lead his blockers and find that extra inch that will allow him to knife through. He seems to have instant acceleration and he also has the strength to break tackles.

> I wouldn't venture to call anyone the greatest running back of all time, because there are too many intangibles involved, but I've never seen any man come to the position with greater gifts.

When O.J. signed one of the most lucrative broadcasting contracts ever with the American Broadcasting Company in 1969, ABC sports director Roone Arledge said of him:

> O.J. Simpson is one of the most versatile young men in sports, not only as an athlete but as a well-informed and articulate spokesman for athletics. We think he has the potential to develop over the years into an outstanding broadcast personality—whether it be as a sports show host, a sports commentator or even as an actor.

> O.J. has said he would like a career in television when his playing days are done and ABC feels he has the long-range potential to become successful in this endeavor.

The ruggedly good-looking Simpson was even more handsome in person than in photographs, and his good looks were complemented by a warm, outgoing personality. "He can walk into a room and suddenly everyone in it is smiling and feeling amiable," said O.J.'s friend Bill Withers. Simpson's charisma commanded attention everywhere.

When O.J. worked on the filming of *Cassandra Crossing* with Sophia Loren, the stunningly beautiful Italian star, she observed that he "cut a dashing figure." And as a television spokesperson for Hertz car rental agency, his likable image and acrobatic dashes

After his retirement from football, Simpson appeared in ads for Hertz rent-a-car. The ad campaign was extremely popular.

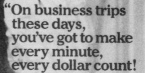

"On business trips these days, you've got to make every minute, every dollar count!

That's why you need Hertz more than ever."

O.J. Simpson

You can depend on Hertz. Hertz has more good people to take care of you, so you can get away fast into a clean, reliable car. More locations. More cars. More kinds of cars. And with Super Saver Rates, you save money, too. With all this, wouldn't you rather rent from Hertz?

The Superstar in rent-a-car.
HERTZ RENTS FORDS AND OTHER FINE CARS.

through airport terminals, leaping over seats, luggage carts, and sundry other hazards, helped to keep his employer number one in the nation in car rentals.

From 1969 to 1976 he earned phenomenal success in each of the foregoing, highly visible ventures, and with success came wealth. But O.J.'s celebrity and prosperity did not come without a price. The collapse of his marriage to Marguerite, under the weight of his frequent absences from home, was perhaps the greatest price that O.J. and, of course, Marguerite, paid for his success. They were divorced in 1979.

Trouble in Troy

Following the Simpsons' divorce for "irreconcilable differences," a reporter for *People* magazine asked Harry Fain, Marguerite's attorney, whether the split had really come as a result of O.J.'s womanizing. Fain replied guardedly, "Frankly, we haven't gone into the reasons for the divorce, but I would say she knew or sensed it." Marguerite later confirmed Fain's appraisal.

Simpson with comediennes Gilda Radner and Jane Curtain while hosting the popular TV series Saturday Night Live. *Simpson's sunny personality brought him several TV appearances.*

DIVORCE AND TRAGEDY

Marguerite Simpson, O.J.'s first wife, hated Buffalo. She thought of it as a dull, drab, eastern industrial city with climatic extremes of heat and cold and a dearth of cultural and recreational attractions. A native Californian, she was tied to her family and friends who were rooted in California. She loved the milder, pleasanter climate of her home state, where she and her children could enjoy their favorite sport of swimming year-round. Marguerite elected to remain in California with Arnelle and Jason, while O.J. maintained a small apartment in Buffalo—not the best arrangement for a healthy marriage.

O.J.'s football career and burgeoning television and movie interests kept him away from home seven or eight months out of any given year. Long periods of separation, along with the pressures of O.J.'s unbridled ambition, played havoc with the Simpsons' relationship, and their marriage bonds started unraveling. In the mid-1970s O.J. himself acknowledged:

> When football is over for the year, it seems like I'm always on the road, making appearances for the companies I work for. . . . All that keeps me on the road and has led to a lot of trouble for us.

> Marguerite and I were apart more than we were together and a marriage can't work when you're separated so much of the time.

For a time, however, it appeared as if the Simpsons might shore up the crumbling foundations of their marriage.

O.J., after long negotiations with the Bills' ownership, arranged to get himself traded to the San Francisco Forty-Niners. The Simpsons then bought a new home in the Brentwood section of Los Angeles, complete with a full-size swimming pool to indulge Marguerite and the children's love of swimming. On September 1, 1977, Marguerite and O.J. had a second daughter, Aaren. Their relationship seemed to be on the mend with the addition of another child, but it was not.

O.J. and Marguerite separated in September of 1978, and O.J. filed for a divorce in March of the following year. Five months later, tragedy struck. On August 18, 1979, the twenty-three-month-old Aaren escaped from her outside playpen and strayed down to the swimming pool. A few minutes later she was found floating facedown in the pool. Aaren was rushed to the UCLA Medical Center, where she lingered in a coma for a week. Aaren Simpson died seven days later, a week before her second birthday.

In their divorce settlement, the Simpsons reportedly split over three million dollars in assets. Marguerite, who had often complained of Simpson's lack of interest in the children, gained custody of Arnelle and Jason. O.J. kept what he called his "dream house" in Brentwood, his permanent residence until June 17, 1994.

In an interview for inclusion in a book called *Superwives*, she told the author, "I have been shoved out of the way, pushed and stepped on by more than one beautiful woman." She candidly admitted feeling "jealous" of—and threatened by—women who shower their affections on celebrities. Marguerite appeared to be directing her comments toward groupies (female fans who follow rock groups or celebrities on tour) in general, but she possibly already felt most endangered by a beauteous blonde closer to home.

Gossip columnists on both coasts first connected Simpson with a tall, blonde named Nicole Brown almost a year before he divorced Marguerite. In reality, they met in June 1977. O.J. started dating the golden-haired beauty from Dana Point, California, almost immediately. To the former Trojan hero, she represented his Helen of Troy.

Smitten by Nicole's grace and beauty, O.J. launched himself without pause into a relationship, with the consummate love experience of his many-rumored affairs behind him. She was eighteen; O.J., twenty-nine. Nicole became the love of O.J.'s life, and he of hers. On April 19, 1979, even though O.J. was still married to Marguerite, the *New York Post* reported that "the Juice" was "still keeping company with his girlfriend Nicole Brown." Their romantic alliance soon became more than just another of O.J.'s affairs.

From love's first stirring, however, O.J. and Nicole, to the early detriment of their relationship, both desperately wanted and needed to totally possess the other. Their consuming passion propelled them to the heights of romantic ecstasy; their uncurbed possessiveness plunged them into the depths of obsessive despair.

O.J. and Nicole finally married on February 2, 1985—nearly six years after his divorce from Marguerite. Close friends and family members viewed their joining with some uneasiness, fearing that the alternating highs and lows of the couple's relationship would inevitably lead to a tragic end to their love affair.

For a time they lived life on the edge, expanding the envelope of pleasures reserved for the rich and famous. They resided sometimes in O.J.'s Brentwood mansion (which he retained as part of the divorce settlement), sometimes in his oceanfront house in Laguna Beach, and still other times in the New York City condominium that O.J. and Nicole bought to accommodate O.J.'s frequent business trips to the East Coast. Nicole relished the swirl and glitter of O.J.'s trendy lifestyle, and O.J. loved showing off his blonde wife in the company of his rich and powerful business associates and friends.

O.J. Simpson and Nicole Brown in 1980, five years before their marriage. Brown began dating Simpson when she was eighteen.

The Simpsons' whirlwind, bicoastal lifestyle slowed down to only occasional flurries of party going and vacationing with the arrival of their daughter, Sydney, the first of the couple's two children, on October 17, 1986. Two years later Nicole and O.J. had a son, Justin, born August 6, 1988. The new family additions did little to alter O.J.'s pattern of pursuing his career interests wherever they took him, which was mostly out of town. Just as he had done during his first marriage, he became an absentee parent. For Nicole, life in the fast lane slowed to a commuter's crawl, as her child-rearing responsibilities kept her home most of the time.

Although the bronze former Trojan and his golden-haired Helen figure continued to maintain their public façade as an ideal married couple, the luster of their seemingly perfect marriage was already starting to wear thin from the abrasions of frequent and prolonged separations—and more. Trouble was brewing in Troy.

Incident at Rockingham

Perhaps no one but O.J. Simpson knows precisely when his second marriage began to show signs of trouble. To this day, many of his closest friends disclaim having had any knowledge—not even the slightest inkling—that all was not right with the Simpsons in their Brentwood paradise. The first indisputable evidence of their domestic discord became known to the public following a New Year's Eve party attended by O.J. and Nicole on December 31, 1988. According to award-winning author Sheila Weller:

> When they got back to Rockingham—both having consumed a good deal of alcohol—they started arguing. Nicole told a close friend that she was angry at having discovered that O.J. had purchased yet another piece of jewelry for [actress] Tawny Kitten (a bracelet this time) [following an earlier gift of earrings] and that she [Nicole] had refused to make love, a reluctance that had been growing ever since she had become worried about contracting AIDS from him.

In the early hours of January 1, 1989, Officers John Edwards and Patricia Milwiski of the Los Angeles Police Department

O.J. and Nicole's home on Rockingham, where police responded to several domestic abuse calls.

responded to a 911 emergency call originating from the Simpson's ivy-covered Brentwood mansion at 360 North Rockingham Avenue. The officers arrived at the estate's Ashford Street gate at about 3:30 A.M. An incident report filed by the investigating officers later that day described what happened shortly after their arrival:

> About that time Nicole Simpson came running out of some bushes near the house. She was wearing only a bra and sweat type pants and she had mud down the r[igh]t leg of her pants. She ran across the driveway to a post containing the gate release button. She collapsed on the post and pushed the button hard several times.

> She was yelling during this time "He's going to kill me, he's going to kill me." [A]s she said this the gate opened and she ran out to me. She grabbed me and hung on to me as she cried nervously and repeated "He's going to kill me."

The soft-spoken Edwards, a patrol training officer, asked Nicole who was going to kill her and she answered, "O.J." Edwards asked her if she meant O.J. Simpson the football player, and she replied yes. Officer Milwiski, a female trainee, reported:

> Nicole Simpson . . . told us that [the suspect] her husband (O.J. Simpson) had beaten her up. She stated that he had slapped her with both open and closed fists, kicked her with his feet, and pulled her hair. Nicole Simpson also stated that suspect (O.J. Simpson) yelled, "I'll kill you."

> [Milwiski also observed] many scratch marks on her neck [and] multiple trauma bruises [including] swollen bruises on her right forehead, scratches on her upper lip [and] a cut on her inner lip.

Officer Edwards added:

> I asked her if [O.J.] had a gun, she said he's got lots of guns. (The question had been for my protection, since she had maintained he was going to kill her.)

> I could see clearly that her face was badly beaten, with a cut lip, swollen and blackened left eye and cheek. I also noted a hand imprint on her left [side of her] neck.

> I saw that she was shaking, so I had my partner put her uniform jacket on Nicole, then had her sit in the back of the police vehicle. As she was giving the crime info to my partner, she kept saying, "You never do anything about him. You talk to him and then leave. I want him arrested, I want him out so I can get my kids." She also made the statement that police have come eight times before for the same thing. . . .

> At about this time O.J. Simpson [clad in a bathrobe] arrived at the closed gate inside the yard.

Simpson began shouting at Nicole in the car and arguing with the police. "I don't want that woman sleeping in my bed anymore," he shouted, "I got two women and I don't want that

One of several police photographs of Nicole after O.J. Simpson had beaten her. As early as 1989, Nicole had expressed fear that O.J. would kill her and get away with it.

woman in my bed anymore." Officer Edwards then informed O.J. that he was going to be placed under arrest for beating Nicole. O.J. replied angrily, "The police has [*sic*] been out here eight times before and now your [*sic*] gonna arrest me for this? This is a family matter. Why do you want to make a big deal of it? We can handle it."

O.J.'s way of handling the situation was to flee. Officer Edwards told O.J. to get dressed and prepare himself for arrest. Once dressed, O.J. slipped past the waiting police and drove out the side electronic gate in his blue 1981 Bentley Turbo Rocket. As reported by Edwards, "He sped off s/b [southbound] Rockingham, 35 to 45 mph." The police gave chase in the predawn hours but failed to catch him. They caught up with Simpson and arrested him later that same day, however, and charged him with assault.

Although Nicole was hospitalized for treatment of multiple injuries, she refused to press charges, presumably to spare O.J. and her children from public embarrassment. Instead, she asked the police to refer the case to the district attorney's office. O.J. eventually pleaded no contest to charges of spousal battery. He was fined $470 and sentenced to 120 hours of community service and two years' probation. The case was recorded as "convicted."

A New Life

The New Year's Day beating suffered by Nicole was only one of many such incidents. In 1985 an LAPD uniformed officer named Mark Fuhrman was called to the Simpson home to break up a domestic dispute in which O.J. Simpson shattered the windshield of Nicole's Mercedes-Benz with a baseball bat.

During a later investigation into Simpson's tendency toward domestic violence conducted by the Los Angeles District Attorney's office, investigators uncovered evidence of sixty-two separate incidents of abuse, manipulation, and threats by Simpson. Deputy District Attorney Christopher Darden wrote:

> [The incidents] began in 1977 (". . . threw her into a wall . . . beat [her] on a corner and in a hotel. . . . 'He continued to beat me as I crawled for the door'"), continued some time around 1982 (". . . said she was hit by Simpson . . . locked her in a wine closet and watched television while she begged . . . backhanded Nicole Simpson across the head, forced her out of a car") and 1986 (". . . beat Nicole Simpson . . . causing . . . a bruise to the head. Simpson . . . told a doctor she was hurt in a bicycle accident").
>
> The 1989 beating, in which she finally called the police, was included, as were several incidents when she told friends that Simpson beat her ("'I really think he's going to kill me,' . . .").

"Later," wrote journalist Tom Elias, "[Nicole] would say in a letter written but never delivered to Simpson that 'I called the cops [New Year's morning] to save my life.'" She further wrote:

> I've never loved you since or been the same. It made me take a look at my life with you—my wonderful life with the Superstar, that wonderful man O.J. Simpson, the father of my kids—that husband of that terribly insecure girl—the girl with no self-esteem or self-worth—and certainly no one could be envious of that life.

Nicole finally garnered sufficient courage to file for divorce in February 1992, citing "irreconcilable differences" (the reason given in O.J.'s divorce from Marguerite). The divorce became final the following October. But Nicole's problems with O.J. did not end with the divorce.

A chronology used later in court indicated that Simpson had begun stalking Nicole in February 1992. In April of that year, he hid in the bushes outside Nicole's rented house on Gretna Green Way and watched while she intimately entertained a male companion. On October 25, 1993, Simpson entered her Gretna Green residence by kicking down the rear door and threatened Nicole orally. Nicole again called 911. A recording of her desperate appeal for help was broadcast countless times after her murder and was heard by millions of appalled listeners the world over.

In January 1994 Nicole moved with her children into a new residence at 875 South Bundy Drive, a condominium purchased with money from her divorce settlement, and attempted to start a new life on her own. "She was *so* happy that she was able to buy the place herself, that she hadn't had to ask for help from anyone,"

The bloody walkway outside Nicole Brown's condo where she and Ron Goldman were found brutally murdered.

said her friend Kris Jenner, wife of Olympic star Bruce Jenner. "I hugged her and said, 'I'm so proud of you!'"

At thirty-five, Nicole had experienced both the breathtaking highs of life among the stars and the doleful lows of domestic discord and abuse. However painful, she had finally garnered the courage to end her seventeen-year relationship with O.J. Simpson. Now, at last, she could look forward to a new life of independence and self-determination. But not for long.

Chapter 1

"Absolutely, 100 Percent Not Guilty"

MANY RESIDENTS OF THE POSH Los Angeles suburb of Brentwood remember the night of June 12, 1994, as a typically balmy spring evening not unlike so many others in Southern California. Yet, before the night ended, a fearsome and bloody double slaying at 875 South Bundy Drive in West Los Angeles would scar the soul of a nation and forever brand that evening different from the rest. Somewhere between 10:00 and 10:30 P.M., in that routinely calm and quiet community, the balefully disturbing yelps of a barking dog heralded the first hint of a perversity in progress.

Screenwriter Pablo Fenjves, who lived near the condominium on Bundy Drive, later reported hearing a dog's "plaintive wail" at approximately 10:15 P.M. Shortly after 10:35 P.M., Stephen Schwab, another neighboring screenwriter, left his home to walk his dog. He soon encountered a white Akita. The dog was barking without letup, and its paws were bloody. Schwab, noticing that the dog lacked identification tags, decided to take the dog in tow until its owner could be found.

Sukru Boztepe, and his wife Bettina Rasmussen, Schwab's neighbors, arrived home at 11:40 P.M. They volunteered to keep the Akita overnight and deliver the dog to the animal shelter in the morning. When the dog became restless in the couple's apartment, they elected to take it for a walk. The Akita led them straight to the gated, shadowy entrance of an upscale condominium

25

at 875 South Bundy Drive. Boztepe's eyes followed along the dimly lit Spanish-tile walkway and fixed upon a woman's body lying in a pool of blood at the end of the walk. It was precisely midnight.

Boztepe and Rasmussen awakened a neighbor, who called the police. Officer Robert Riske of the Los Angeles Police Department arrived at the crime scene at 12:09 A.M. He found the body of a young blonde woman with multiple slashings and stab wounds, curled in a fetal position at the foot of a flight of stairs. In the bushes, ten feet from the woman's body, he discovered the body of a young man with similar wounds.

Officer Riske then entered the residence through a door left slightly ajar and found two small children asleep upstairs. Back outside, he found bloody footprints leading to an alley behind the condominium. He called for backup. Additional officers arrived and cordoned off the area with crime-scene tape. And the hunt for a double murderer began.

A shot of the bloody walkway after Nicole's murder gives silent testimony to the savagery of the crime—Nicole's neck was slashed so deeply that her spinal cord was visible.

O.J. Not a Suspect

"[O.J.'s] marriage to Nicole Brown, a blonde all-American beauty," wrote Linda Deutsch, the Associated Press's premier courtroom reporter, "was an interracial union that seemed made in heaven." Deutsch continued:

> Nothing bad could ever happen to this golden couple. And then the worst thing possible happened.
>
> In the warm darkness of a June night, on a street in trendy Brentwood, the blood of Nicole Brown Simpson flowed like a river down the pathway of her California condominium. Her beautiful swan-like neck had been slashed open by the knife of a killer—a gash so vicious it nearly decapitated her. Nearby, another body lay oozing blood. Ronald Goldman, a waiter on a mission to deliver a pair of eyeglasses, became the accidental victim in one of the most gruesome murders to grip the public consciousness in decades.
>
> Could O.J. be the killer? No one wanted to believe it. . . . And for five days, it seemed that not even the police could believe it. They interviewed Simpson, took a sample of his blood but did not arrest him. The investigation continued.

LAPD detective Mark Fuhrman, as he would later testify, received a call at home at about 1:05 A.M. on June 13 to proceed to 875 South Bundy. He arrived at Bundy at 2:10 A.M., shortly after Ron Phillips, the first detective on the scene. Fuhrman, a strapping six-foot-three-inch former Marine Corps machine gunner in Vietnam, walked through the condominium and found nothing disturbed. From the balcony, however, he spotted a knit cap, one leather glove, and a trail of bloody footprints leading toward the side alley.

Detective Philip Vannatter of the LAPD's Robbery-Homicide Division arrived on the scene at approximately 4:30 A.M. At age fifty-three, the big, strong, sandy-haired Vannatter was a

Los Angeles police detective Mark Fuhrman found a knit cap and a bloody glove at Nicole's condo.

well-respected, twenty-eight-year veteran of the LAPD. He took charge of the investigation. Detective Tom Lange arrived a half hour later. Deputy District Attorney Christopher Darden described Lange as "an interesting guy" who "really complemented his partner, Phil Vannatter."

By the time Vannatter arrived, Nicole had been identified as the former wife of O.J. Simpson. Officers on the scene informed Vannatter that Nicole's children had been found asleep and unharmed upstairs. Vannatter, according to his later testimony, elected to proceed at once to Simpson's Rockingham house to "make a notification" to the dead woman's former husband and to arrange for the "disposition" of the two small children. He stressed that O.J. Simpson was not a suspect at that time.

A Hero in Handcuffs

The four detectives arrived at 360 North Rockingham Avenue shortly after 5:00 A.M. They saw lights on in the house, but they received no answer when they rang the intercom buzzer at the Ashford Street gate. Detective Fuhrman then discovered a speck of blood on the driver's side door handle of a white Ford Bronco parked askew near the estate's Rockingham entrance. Fuhrman informed Vannatter, who later said:

> We were within five minutes of a very brutal murder scene. I knew it was connected with Mr. Simpson because his ex-wife was one of the victims. I became

concerned we might have another murder scene, or someone injured inside. So we decided to go over the wall [without benefit of a search warrant]. I was looking for people, not evidence.

Vannatter, however, called for a criminalist (one who collects, catalogs, analyzes, and preserves evidence) and directed Fuhrman, the most athletic of the four detectives, to scale the five-foot wall and unlock the gate for the others to enter. The detectives rang the bell at the front door and again received no answer.

At about 5:30 A.M. they walked around to the guest quarters located to the right rear of the main house and knocked on the doors of Simpson's daughter Arnelle and houseguest Brian "Kato" Kaelin. Arnelle informed the detectives that her father had flown to Chicago the previous night on business. She admitted them to the house and tried to reach her father by telephone.

Meanwhile, Detective Fuhrman was questioning Kato Kaelin and learned that Kaelin had heard three mysterious thumps on his rear wall the night before at around 10:40. Between 6:00 and 6:15 A.M., Fuhrman went alone to the rear of Kaelin's quarters to investigate the possible cause of the thumps and discovered a bloody right-handed glove on the backyard path between the guest wing wall and the fence along the property line. During the next forty minutes, Fuhrman summoned the other detectives back one at a time to view

The mate to the bloody glove found at Nicole's condo was discovered at Simpson's Los Angeles home by L.A. police officers.

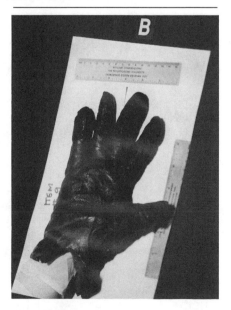

his finding. It was later determined that the right-handed glove at Rockingham matched the left-handed glove found at Bundy.

Shortly after daybreak, Detective Vannatter discovered drops of blood leading from the Bronco to the front door of the house. At approximately 7:00 A.M. Vannatter called in for a search warrant and ordered the house sealed off as an official crime scene—two hours after the police entered the estate without a warrant. The detectives continued their search inside the house.

Arnelle finally located her father in Chicago by telephone, and Detective Ron Phillips advised Simpson of his ex-wife's murder. Simpson returned to Los Angeles that morning and was briefly handcuffed at his home. Before accompanying police downtown for questioning at about noon, a grim-faced O.J. said, "I know nothing."

Putting a Rumor to Rest

Asked by reporters if Simpson was a suspect, LAPD commander David Gascon said, "We are not going to rule anyone out. Obviously we will be interviewing everyone that we think is remotely involved in this case. Everyone is a witness at this point."

Simpson talked with Detectives Phil Vannatter and Tom Lange in a taped interview lasting some three-and-a-half hours.

The detectives observed a cut on O.J.'s left middle finger. Simpson explained that he had cut himself on a glass tumbler that he broke in the bathroom of his Chicago hotel when notified of Nicole's murder by Detective Lange.

An L.A. police department photo reveals the cut on Simpson's middle finger. Expert testimony by the prosecution and the defense was unable to dismiss or affirm Simpson's broken glass explanation.

Throughout the questioning, O.J. maintained his innocence and denied knowing anything about the murders of his wife and her friend Ron. He left police headquarters late in the day with his attorney, Howard Weitzman, who told reporters: "We are done for the day. We came here to cooperate. We did that. There is a continuing investigation. If we are asked to come back, we intend to cooperate." Shielding his weary forty-six-year-old client from a barrage of questions from members of the press, Weitzman explained: "He is in shock, he is devastated. He had a tremendous amount of feeling for Nicole. . . . It's a tremendous loss."

Attorney Robert L. Shapiro, one of the first lawyers retained by Simpson to defend him against murder charges.

The next day, Tuesday, June 14, O.J. retained the services of Los Angeles attorney Robert L. Shapiro—renown for representing such celebrity clients as Christian Brando, Daryll Strawberry, Vince Coleman, and others. Weitzman, who specialized in civil cases, stepped aside on June 15, stating that given both his close personal relationship with Simpson and his own professional commitments he felt it best to withdraw.

This change of counsel posed a question as to whether a lawyer should represent a personal friend. By his action, Howard Weitzman had answered no. Others were not so inclined. "Of all the dozens of lawyers who would be involved in the so-called 'Trial of the Century," wrote journalist Tom Elias, "no others had similar qualms." As an example, Elias quoted Robert Shapiro:

"I didn't hesitate for a moment when I was called," Robert Shapiro told me [Elias] during the fall of 1994.

Shapiro headed Simpson's defense team until it became clear there would be no plea bargain, that the case would go to trial. But Cochran [Johnnie Cochran Jr., who would later become Simpson's lead defense counsel] and Weitzman hesitated. An old Simpson pal who had played tennis with O.J. for years and watched most of the football games he played at the University of Southern California, Weitzman was the first lawyer Simpson called. But he bowed out of the case when it was just two days old, bouncing it over to friend Shapiro. Weitzman . . . accompanied Simpson to police headquarters in downtown Los Angeles the day after the murders, but became visibly upset when Simpson insisted on talking alone to homicide detectives Philip Vannatter and Tom Lange. Rumors—never confirmed—circulated for months that Weitzman quit the next day not out of pique over being crossed by his client,

O.J. Simpson leaves the headquarters of the L.A. police with attorney Howard Weitzman (left) after volunteering to be questioned by police.

but because Simpson confessed the crimes to him. Weitzman has never revealed what Simpson told him in private, but publicly insisted that he couldn't defend Simpson because their friendship was too old and too close.

Robert Shapiro supported Weitzman's public pronouncement. "There were rumors at the time that the reason Weitzman left the case was that O.J had made a confession to him," he wrote later. "That is categorically not true." Human nature being what it is, however, such rumors are hard to put to rest—categorically or otherwise.

Sealed Lips

Separate funeral services were held for Nicole Brown Simpson and Ronald Lyle Goldman on Thursday, June 16. O.J. Simpson and his children attended an eleven o'clock service for Nicole at St. Martin of Tours Catholic Church in Brentwood. Author Sheila Weller wrote:

> Simpson and his children took seats in a front pew, with the Brown family. "My mommy's in there!" Justin said as Nicole's flower-draped casket was wheeled in. "That's funny. What's she doing in there?" Justin did not seem to understand his mother's death. He twitched around and laughed, as confused children at funerals do. Sydney was more solemn. Her father spent most of the service comfortingly stroking her long, golden brown hair.
>
> Reverend Monsignor Lawrence O'Leary ascended the pulpit and addressed the departed's "grieving husband." According to some guests, the monsignor seemed to have geared his entire sermon toward Simpson. We must keep ourselves clear and clean in the eyes of God, the priest declared. We must treat others with respect and kindness. We can't have any dark spots on our consciences. . . .
>
> Denise and Tanya stepped to the pulpit and spoke about their sister's hope and spirit. Kris Jenner started crying

uncontrollably. When the Brown sisters exclaimed, "We love you, Nicole! We miss you!," everyone in the church began to cry. . . .

But the most significant remark made during the whole funeral was one that Simpson's just-resigned attorney Howard Weitzman made, after the church service, to a close friend of the Browns. Simpson had requested that Sydney and Justin be brought to see him for a few hours.

"Whatever you do," Weitzman said now, "do *not* let the kids go back up to O.J.'s."

O.J. with children Sydney and Justin at Nicole Brown's funeral.

Weitzman said the words gravely but matter-of-factly, "As if," said the person he was addressing, "he had something important to tell me that he knew that I knew he could not say."

Information disclosed to an attorney by a client is privileged and protected by law from public exposure. The public will never know what moved Weitzman to issue such a warning. His lips were sealed forever by attorney-client privilege.

A Plea and a Gesture

At 8:30 A.M. on Friday, June 17, Detective Tom Lange telephoned attorney Robert Shapiro and said, "We are going to charge O.J. Simpson with two counts of first-degree murder. We want you to surrender him here by ten o'clock."

"I'll contact him immediately and make the arrangements," Shapiro replied, "and we'll be bringing him in to turn himself in voluntarily." But he spoke too soon.

"When the time came for him to be arrested on June 17, 1994," wrote AP correspondent Linda Deutsch, "O.J. Simpson did what he was famous for—he ran." Deutsch continued:

> With his friend A.C. Cowlings at the wheel of a white Bronco, a distraught Simpson led police—and America—on a bizarre, televised slow-speed chase that wound its way 60 miles across Southern California freeways and set the theme for his trial to come. Justice would be slow, filled with bizarre moments, and all of it would be televised for a public that could not take their eyes off it.
>
> The man at center stage, who had sent what looked like a suicide note to the world before he fled, came back, surrendered and decided to fight the charges with all the might and money at his disposal.

Simpson's white Ford Bronco, driven by friend Al Cowlings during the slow-speed chase after Simpson was charged with murder. Later, police found a disguise, a passport, and a suicide note written by Simpson inside the car.

A SUICIDE NOTE?

At a news conference held on June 17, 1994, Robert Kardashian, an attorney and Simpson's longtime friend, chokingly read what many thought to be O.J.'s suicide note to reporters and television audiences around the world. Robert Shapiro, Simpson's attorney, later included the entire text of the note in his book *The Search for Justice*. Parts of the note are shown herein:

> To whom it may concern: First, everyone understand, I have nothing to do with Nicole's murder. I loved her. I always have and I always will. If we had a problem, it's because I loved her so much.

> Recently we came to an understanding that for now we were not right for each other, at least for now. Despite our love we were different and that's why we mutually agreed to go our separate ways. . . .

> Unlike what has been written in the press, Nicole and I had a great relationship for most of our lives together. . . . I don't want to belabor knocking the press, but I can't believe what is being said. Most of it is totally made up. I know you have a job to do, but as a last wish, please, please, please, leave my children in peace. Their lives will be tough enough. . . .

> I think of my life and feel I've done most of the right things, so why do I end up like this? I can't go on. No matter what the outcome people will look and point. I can't take that. I can't subject my children to that. This way they can move on and go on with their lives. Please, if I've done anything worthwhile in my life, let my kids live in peace from you, the press.

> I've had a good life. I'm proud of how I lived. My mother taught me to do unto others. I treated people the way I wanted to be treated. I've always tried to be up and helpful. So why is this happening? I'm sorry for the Goldman family. I know how much it hurts. . . .

> Don't feel sorry for me. I've had a great life, great friends. Please think of the real O.J. and not this lost person.

> Thanks for making my life special. I hope I helped yours.

> Peace and love, O.J.

Simpson signed the note with a happy face drawn within his "O," which prompted a later comment from Deputy District Attorney Christopher Darden. In his book *In Contempt*, Darden wrote, "A suicide note with a happy face. *Right.*"

On July 8, following a six-day preliminary hearing that offered a preview of the prosecution case, municipal judge Kathleen Kennedy-Powell returned her ruling that there was "ample evidence" to bind O.J. Simpson over for trial. Judge Kennedy-Powell ordered Simpson to appear in court two weeks later for formal arraignment.

On July 22, O.J. Simpson returned to court to plead to the charges against him. "When the door to his holding cell opened," wrote Linda Deutsch, "and the TV camera rolled, it was clear that Simpson knew he was on." Deutsch went on to write:

Simpson is photographed by the police after being booked for murder.

> Asked for his plea in the June 12 slashing deaths of ex-wife Nicole Brown Simpson, 35, and her friend Ron Goldman, 25, the former sports star and actor delivered his one line with feeling: "Absolutely, 100 percent not guilty."

As Simpson was escorted back to his holding cell, he gestured with a thumbs-up sign to friends in the spectator section and—via the magic of television satellites—to a worldwide audience.

Chapter 2

The People v. Orenthal James Simpson

O N JULY 22, 1994, O.J. SIMPSON was bound over for trial on two counts of murder, with a provision that permitted the death penalty. On that same day, the state of California assigned superior court judge Lance A. Ito to the Simpson case. Pretrial preparations and posturing by both the prosecution and the defense commenced immediately and absorbed the remaining months of 1994.

The Judge

Judge Lance Ito is a light-spirited, learned jurist with a solid legal background. His Japanese-American heritage made him a perfect choice to preside without bias over a trial that would soon become sullied with racial undertones. A *Newsweek* article written by Mark Miller with Jeanne Gordon, and shown here in part, provided this profile of Ito:

> A third-generation Japanese-American whose parents were interned in a Wyoming detention camp during World War II, Ito went to UCLA and Berkeley's Boalt Hall School of Law. He became an assistant district attorney in Los Angeles County in 1977, volunteering for a hard-charging prosecutorial team assigned to gang-related crimes. The team racked up an impressive conviction rate, and Ito, a tireless worker, went on to higher things. He was appointed to the bench in 1987 and pro-

moted to Superior Court in 1989. In 1992, after presiding at the trial of megabucks savings-and-loan swindler Charles Keating, Ito was named Trial Judge of the Year by the Los Angeles County Bar Association.

The *Newsweek* article revealed that although Ito presides over serious matters from his superior court bench, he has been known by his colleagues to engage in occasional flights of fancy.

Those who know him well say Ito's stern judicial bearing conceals a mischievous sense of humor. San Diego lawyer Robert D. Rose, who went to UCLA with Ito in the 1970s, remembers Ito running through the dorm yelling "Banzai!" on the anniversary of Pearl Harbor Day—wearing nothing but an antique leather flying helmet. Deputy district attorney Peter S. Berman says Ito is a relentless prankster who livened up the L.A. prosecutors' long hours with practical jokes. "You could come in and find all your furniture going up and down repeatedly on the freight elevator. It's funny but immature—it was the kind of stuff we did just to alleviate the stress of dealing with the murderers of children everyday," Berman says.

Judge Lance Ito was criticized throughout the trial for allowing the lawyers to posture and spend too much time interviewing witnesses.

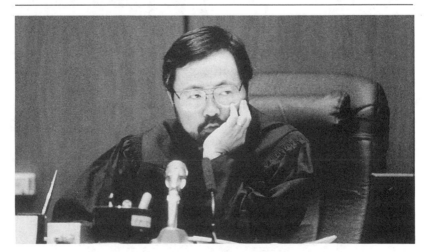

Ito's penchant for pranks, however, in no way lessens his serious approach to his judicial calling, as Miller and Gordon indicated:

> But friends also say Ito, 44, has never forgotten the Japanese-American internment, and that his parents' humiliation during that time helps explain both his fairness as a judge and his fierce drive to succeed. "One of the reasons I try to do as good a job as I can [is that] I don't want to cause problems for my parents," Ito told KCBS[-TV]. "There have been some of the pundits [critics] who have said things that have been critical of my performance in some high-profile cases, and naturally, that wounds my parents deeply."

In the weeks and months ahead, the pundits would come out in full voice—gushing torrents of words that wound.

The Prosecutors

Los Angeles district attorney Gil Garcetti appointed two veteran assistants, William Hodgman and Marcia Clark, to head the prosecution team. Hodgman's likable, soft-spoken style suggested a likely counterbalance to co-prosecutor Clark's more strident courtroom demeanor.

Reporting for *People* magazine, writers David Ellis and Lyndon Stambler described the tall, balding Hodgman as "a low-key but tenacious attorney known for his ability to keep juries focused on the facts." In a brief profile of the forty-two-year-old prosecutor, Ellis and Stambler wrote:

> Hodgman developed his steely courtroom persona during more than 100 prosecutions. . . . [He] grew up in the L.A. suburb La Habra, earned his law degree at the University of California's Hastings College of the Law in San Francisco in 1978 and joined the Los Angeles district attorney's office as a junior prosecutor. . . .
>
> As the $120,000-a-year chief of the district attorney's Bureau of Central Operations, Hodgman handled the 1993 investigation into sexual molestation charges

against Michael Jackson. Between trials, he unwinds by playing guitar with the Assassins, a group of amateur rockers from the D.A.'s office. ("I'm sure it's probably painful for him to hear this, but he's not very good," confides L.A. defense attorney Michael Yamamoto. "The only time I saw him get really wild and excitable was at a Bruce Springsteen concert.")

Despite his experience and unflappable approach to the law, the rigors of prosecuting a high-profile celebrity case would soon take a heavy toll on Hodgman, and Christopher Darden, a seasoned black prosecutor, would replace him early in the trial.

Darden, raised in a poor, working-class neighborhood in Richmond, California, worked his way through San Jose State University. He went on to earn his law degree at the University of California's Hastings College of the Law in San Francisco at the same time Bill Hodgman was there. Darden followed his calling to the Los Angeles District Attorney's office and spent fifteen years prosecuting murderers, drug dealers, gang members, and racist cops. In addition to his duties as a deputy district attorney,

Prosecutor Marcia Clark (left) and Deputy District Attorney William Hodgman on the second day of the Simpson trial. Hodgman dropped out of the trial after being hospitalized for chest pains.

Prosecutor Christopher Darden received a lot of criticism from the black community for his role in the Simpson trial.

Darden teaches as an associate professor of law at Southwestern University School of Law in Los Angeles.

Associated Press journalist Linda Deutsch described Darden as "a black prosecutor whose race made him a lightning rod for attacks by Johnnie L. Cochran Jr., the hard-ball playing defense attorney who was also black." Deutsch wrote:

Cochran, once a mentor and friend to Darden, accused the district attorney of choosing the younger man for the case merely because of his race. Their friendship soured and broke into outright warfare when Darden tried to ban the use of the word "nigger" in the trial [so as not to inflame a predominantly black jury], losing out to Cochran's argument that race was an issue that could not be avoided.

From day two of the trial, the bulk of the prosecution's burden to prove O.J. Simpson's guilt "beyond a reasonable doubt" would rest equally on the shoulders of Darden and co-prosecutor Marcia Clark.

"Marcia Clark," wrote her biographer Clifford L. Linedecker, "was propelled into instant celebrity when she stepped into the spotlight as a lead prosecutor of former-football-star-turned-Hollywood-actor O.J. Simpson on twin murder charges." Linedecker then asked:

So, just who is Marcia Clark, the bright-eyed, frizzy-haired forty-one-year-old woman on whose narrow shoulders rests so much responsibility?

Among her colleagues with the D.A.'s Office, she is recognized and respected as a tough, hard-hitting prosecutor who has repeatedly proven her ability to deliver victories in difficult homicide cases that are often incredibly complicated. She is a battle-tested veteran of celebrity trials [for example, in 1991, Marcia successfully prosecuted sitcom star Rebecca Schaeffer's murderer, Robert John Bardo] whose skills and unique dedication to her job are undebatable.

She is unintimidated by the prospect of squaring off in a crowded courtroom before television cameras and millions of spectators around the world, against such high-profile defense attorneys as Robert L. Shapiro, Johnnie Cochran, and F. Lee Bailey.

To some observers she is the aggressive, hard-edged, in-your-face woman [soon to be] seen and heard daily on television, exchanging sarcastic barbs, accusations, and insults, verbal-punch by verbal-punch with the famous defendant's "dream team" of high-paid defense lawyers. . . .

Her dazzling courtroom accomplishments, however, represent only one aspect of her multifaceted and intricately fascinating life and personality. . . . She is a twice-divorced single mother [of two boys] who shops at bargain stores and attends wedding showers with her girlfriends, takes her sons to the park to play, and consumes mystery and suspense novels by the stack. . . .

"She is an incredibly hard worker," [Los Angeles D.A. Gil Garcetti] says. "She's married to the District Attorney's Office," he told journalists.

Marcia Clark, a 1979 graduate of Southwestern School of Law in Los Angeles, would need to call on every ounce of her energy, wits, and dedication in her coming clash with O.J. Simpson's "dream team."

The Dream Team

Although O.J. Simpson had not been charged with a crime or even declared a suspect when Robert Shapiro took over the reins as O.J.'s new defense counsel, he immediately set about organizing a group of some of the most distinguished defense attorneys and criminal experts in the nation. "The primary challenge to the defense is to anticipate the prosecution's case," Shapiro wrote later. He followed with an explanation of his defense strategy:

> Since I'm not at all reluctant to admit that I don't know everything, I seek out other professionals who can think like the prosecution with me. When I'm putting together a defense team, I try to find the most credible experts—people who ordinarily and often testify for the prosecution and are or have been employed by government agencies. These people not only gain the respect of the jury, but my getting them keeps the "top of the line" experts out of the hands of the prosecution.
>
> We have to find out what the police know, and do what they're doing as they're doing it. And not only must we do what they're doing, we must do things they *should* be doing but for whatever reason aren't. Most important, they make mistakes, and we have to find out what those mistakes are. *Fast.*

Included in Shapiro's eminent assemblage were Alan Dershowitz, Harvard University law professor; F. Lee Bailey, famed criminal attorney; Dr. Michael Baden, noted pathologist and director of the Forensic Sciences Unit of the New York State Police; Gerald Uelmen, retired dean of Santa Clara University Law School; and Dr. Henry Lee, esteemed forensic scientist and director of the State Forensic Science Laboratory in Connecticut. Johnnie Cochran Jr., Los Angeles's most respected black attorney, joined the group later at Simpson's request.

To aid in the defense investigation, Shapiro engaged the services of private investigator Bill Pavelic, a retired nineteen-year veteran of the LAPD. "Pavelic misses nothing," Shapiro wrote.

*The Simpson Dream Team—
(clockwise) F. Lee Bailey,
Alan Dershowitz, Robert
Shapiro, Johnnie Cochran, and
Barry Scheck.*

"Not only can he find the needle in the haystack, he can tell you who dropped it there and when." Nor was Pavelic the only investigator contracted by Shapiro. "At [F. Lee] Bailey's recommendation, I quickly contacted Pat McKenna, an affable former Vietnam vet and experienced private investigator based in Palm Beach," continued Shapiro. "Another investigator, Barry Hostetler, came on board at the urging of my old friend [famed defense attorney] Gerry Spence."

Shapiro knew that the prosecution would rely heavily on DNA (deoxyribonucleic acid, often described as the "building block" or "genetic fingerprint" of human beings) evidence in attempting to link Simpson to the crime scene. To counter the prosecution's use of DNA, Shapiro added New York attorneys Barry Scheck and Peter Neufeld, both pioneers in the evidentiary use of DNA. "It wasn't long," wrote Shapiro, "before the office staff had dubbed the New Yorkers Simon and Garfunkel."

Whatever and whomever Shapiro needed, Shapiro got. As the ranks of O.J. defenders swelled quickly to a formidable force, it must have seemed to the prosecution that Shapiro was attempting to hire, in the Hollywood phrasing, a cast of thousands. He at least seemed to be sparing no effort or expense in garnering his team.

The media, as if covering a sporting event, lost no time in dubbing O.J.'s prestigious defense group the Dream Team. But this was hardly just another football game or athletic event. Two people had been brutally murdered. And O.J. Simpson, the accused perpetrator, was about to stand trial for the crime.

The Jury

Both the prosecution and defense teams spent the summer and fall of 1994 engaged in separate but equally intense efforts to prepare for the impending trial. On September 9, prosecutors announced that they would forgo the death penalty and instead seek life without parole for Simpson.

Jury selection began on September 26 and ended on November 3. A jury of eight women and four men—eight blacks, one white, one Hispanic, and two people of mixed race—was impaneled.

FOUR STEPS TO JURY SELECTION

In *The O.J. Simpson Trial in Black and White*, a book written by journalists Tom Elias and Dennis Schatzman, Elias explained the four-step jury selection process:

> The jury that eventually acquitted Simpson never came near to reflecting the ethnic mix in Los Angeles County, where Simpson lived and where his ex-wife Nicole and her friend Ronald Goldman were murdered. . . . The final jury was composed of nine African Americans, two Caucasians and one Latino.
>
> This came about via a four-step process starting with [District Attorney Gil] Garcetti's first major decision in the case—to gun for a grand jury indictment, thus avoiding a preliminary hearing on the evidence. . . . Garcetti's move all but guaranteed that Simpson's jury would feature at least a few blacks.
>
> Step two in getting a mostly minority jury was the hardship questionnaire administered by [Judge] Ito. It eliminated anyone whose employer would not continue paying wages for the unlimited time required in the Simpson case. It meant jurors would likely be government employees, postal workers or persons employed by large corporations that could afford to share the cost of civic duty. . . .
>
> The third step toward a mostly black jury was an intensive questioning process that began when potential jurors not eliminated by hardship filled out a 294-entry questionnaire designed by lawyers and consultants for both sides. . . .
>
> The judge excused any who admitted knowing much about Simpson or his case, along with all who admitted having experience with domestic abuse and those who said they would dislike being sequestered. This meant that anyone with a high degree of literacy was bound to be bounced, because it was impossible in the months leading up to the trial to read any newspaper or magazine without learning something about the case. . . .
>
> The final selection step allowed peremptory challenges, when lawyers summarily and without needing to provide explanation dismissed 34 jurors and alternates who had survived the questioning process. Race became a major and obvious factor in the trial only during the last two steps of jury selection. . . .

The four steps to jury selection outlined by Elias ultimately led to a jury where three-quarters of its members were black. And in a prosecution case requiring heavy reliance on forensic science and complex DNA analyses, the four-step process impaneled only two jurors with better than a high school education.

The jury assembly room in the downtown Los Angeles courthouse. Each potential juror answered a 294-entry questionnaire.

"As soon as I became a member of the Simpson [prosecution] team," wrote Christopher Darden, "I immediately read each of the first twelve jurors' questionnaires and the transcripts of their voir dire, the in-court questioning by lawyers. I didn't like what I saw." The outspoken prosecutor explained why:

> Certainly, I was concerned about the racial makeup of the jury, but not because of my father's prediction that blacks wouldn't convict Simpson. I was still clinging to my belief that blacks had such a strong sense of morality and justice that they would convict once they saw the overwhelming evidence against Simpson.
>
> No, I was more concerned by the rumor that Johnnie Cochran had said, "Just give me one black on that jury." It was clear that their jury consultant [Jo-Ellan Dimetrius] had pushed for the kind of panel that we ended up with, mostly black, with little education beyond high school. It wasn't that I didn't want black jurors. But Cochran had made it clear that this was going

to be a case based on the fact that O.J. Simpson was black. I was offended by that from the beginning and I could see how destructive this case could be. Anyone who has truly fought for racial equality in the justice system hated to see those issues manipulated to fit an accused double murderer who—for years—had done everything he could to remove himself from the black community and had actually received *coddling* from the LAPD. They had practically looked the other way while the man beat his wife! And now, Cochran and the rest of Simpson's lawyers were going to say that O.J. had been framed? They were going to claim that this was about racial prejudice? That's what a predominantly black jury meant; more encouragement for Cochran to take this case away from the two slaughtered victims, to cry wolf with every civil rights issue and turn a murder case into a bogus retribution for past injustices.

But race wasn't the only problem with this panel. Only a couple of jurors had college degrees, even though we were planning to rely heavily on a relatively new, incredibly complex kind of forensics—DNA. [Forensics is a science that deals with the relation and application of medical facts to legal problems.] One juror was an employee of Hertz Corporation, the company Simpson had shilled [been a spokesman] for during the last decade. I couldn't believe some of these people had slipped through voir dire.

When I brought up my questions about the jury to Bill [Hodgman] and Marcia [Clark], they were understandably defensive [since they had participated in picking the jury].

"They were the best of the lot," Bill said, rubbing his close-cropped beard. "If you think they're bad, you ought to see the ones who were coming up." So I read the questionnaires of the juror candidates who were to be questioned next. They were incredible.

Darden cited numerous examples of juror candidates with racial biases and axes to grind with the police and the justice system. At best, the remaining juror candidates were not of a sort that any prosecutor hoping for a conviction would tend to choose. The seating of twelve alternate jurors drawn from that pool completed jury selection. The alternates comprised nine women and three men—seven blacks, four whites, and one Hispanic.

"That was the jury we were given, the one we helped select," Darden wrote summarily, "and as October faded into November and the trial loomed around the corner, there wasn't time to bemoan the fact that we were going to have to convince jurors who probably didn't like us and already discounted our case."

A New Leader

On January 11, 1995, with the jurors sequestered, the court released volatile prosecution documents accusing Simpson of beating, debasing, and stalking Nicole during their seventeen-year relationship. The defense moved to bar all evidence of domestic violence, accusing the prosecution of character assassination. A compromise was reached when the prosecution withdrew eighteen of sixty-two abuse allegations. But hearings on evidence admissibility—especially DNA evidence—continued with the jury absent from the courtroom, as they would throughout the trial.

On January 11, Judge Ito released two jurors from the panel. "One was a Latina letter carrier who was reportedly in an abusive relationship," wrote Robert Shapiro, "the other, the African-American man who worked for Hertz." The alternate jury pool then stood at ten.

A week later, following a sharp strategy disagreement among defense attorneys, Johnnie Cochran took over as lead counsel for the defense team on January 18. Prosecution fears that O.J.'s defenders intended to play the so-called race card could scarcely have been eased by Cochran's takeover of the Dream Team.

Opening statements in *The People of the State of California v. Orenthal James Simpson* were then scheduled for January 24.

Chapter 3

"This Is Not a Racial Issue"

ON JANUARY 24, 1995, DEPUTY District Attorney Christopher Darden opened the people's case against Simpson, concentrating on the renown defendant's motive. Darden, the sole black member of the prosecution team in a case ridden with racial undertones, was assigned to portray Simpson as a wife beater and abuser. It would fall to co-prosecutor Marcia Clark to establish a timeline and the wherewithal enabling Simpson to have committed the double murder. Darden later recounted the opening moments:

> I stood, greeted the jury, and set out trying to explain to them why this man killed his wife, why he'd risk everything because of his obsession.

> You think, "Why would he do it? Not the O.J. Simpson we've all known for years." But that leads to another question: do you really know O.J. Simpson? Because what we've been seeing is the public face, the public persona, the athlete, the actor.

> But like many men, he has a private face as well, the face that Nicole Brown saw every day and the same face that Nicole Brown and Ronald Goldman faced in the last moments of their lives, the face of a wife beater, abuser, controller.

51

He killed Nicole for a single reason—one as old as himself—jealousy. . . . He could not stand losing her and so he murdered her. In his mind, she belonged to him. And if he couldn't have her, no one could.

Darden told the jurors that Simpson obsessively controlled Nicole during their seven-year marriage—and afterward. He smashed in the windshield of her Mercedes-Benz with a baseball bat in 1985, Darden said, and struck her savagely during an argument on January 1, 1989. Darden further told how Simpson stalked Nicole after their breakup in 1992 and how he spied on her and a male friend during a romantic liaison in Nicole's Bundy Drive condominium.

And as for Ron Goldman, he "simply got in the way."

"Motive, Physical Evidence, Opportunity"

Darden then yielded the lectern to Deputy District Attorney Marcia Clark, who addressed the opportunity and means available to the defendant. Utilizing gory photographs of the crime scene outside Nicole's condominium and at Simpson's estate, Clark traced a "trail of blood" from South Bundy Drive to the North Rockingham location. Darden summarized her presentation this way:

[Simpson's] blood was at the scene, confirmed by both DNA and conventional serology [a science dealing with serums, especially their reactions and properties]. "Matches the defendant," Marcia intoned, flipping from photograph to photograph of blood drops outside Nicole Brown's condominium. "Matches the defendant." Click. "Matches the defendant." Click. "Matches the defendant." Click. . . .

There was a cut on the middle finger of his left hand, consistent with the blood drops at the scene. There were bloody footprints at the scene: size 12. His size. Bruno Maglis, $160 loafers. His shoes. There was one bloody glove at the scene of the murder[s]. His glove. Another bloody glove at his house. His glove. There was blood in

The blood-covered walkway outside Nicole's condo. Nicole's blood was also found in Simpson's car and at his home.

his bathroom, in his foyer, in his Bronco. The blood in his Bronco came from three different people and two of them were lying dead in front of Nicole Brown's condo. [The third blood sample matched Simpson's blood.] Nicole's blood was mingled with Ron Goldman's on Goldman's boot.

"Blood is where blood should not be," Marcia said in that voice that fascinated me—firm and feminine at the same time. There was hair and fiber evidence, she said, including a hair on Ronald Goldman that matched Simpson's, a man he'd never met before the murder[s].

Simpson had no alibi. And there was proof that he was on the road just before the murders. Cellular phone records showed calls from Simpson at 10:02 and 10:03 P.M. to his girlfriend, Paula Barbieri. He was driving around in the Bronco, trying to reach Paula ten or fifteen minutes before the murder[s]. It was an incredible case—motive, physical evidence, opportunity.

DNA analyses indicated that blood droplets found near bloody footprints on the walkway to Nicole's condominium matched the defendant's blood. Bloodstains on socks discovered in Simpson's bedroom were compatible with the blood of both Simpson and Nicole. And a test of blood from a glove found beside his Brentwood mansion revealed a mixture consistent with the blood of Simpson and the victims.

"When one [test] after another after another after another comes back to the same person," Clark concluded, "then you realize the test is accurate."

"A Loving Family Man"

Defense counsel Johnnie Cochran Jr. disagreed. In his opening comments, Cochran promised the jury that DNA experts would testify for the defense and refute the accuracy of the prosecution's tests. The defense would also point out what the black defender called "the lack of integrity of the prosecution's evidence." Cochran claimed that collection of evidence had been mishandled from the start, and he accused the district attorney's office of committing "a rush to judgment."

The defense, Cochran said, would produce evidence that shows blood taken from under Nicole's fingernails is of a differ-

Police photographs of the bloody footprints found on the walkway outside Nicole's condo. The footprints matched Simpson's shoe size and the type of shoe he wore.

Simpson with lawyers Cochran and Shapiro at the trial. Simpson's lawyers eventually postulated a theory that Simpson had been framed by the L.A. police department.

ent type than Simpson's. And they would bring forth witnesses that would provide Simpson with an irrefutable alibi.

The polished, smooth-talking defender went on to portray Simpson as a loving family man who had always maintained a "circle of benevolence." Defense counsel Robert Shapiro later wrote:

> Johnnie described O.J.'s longtime love for and generosity to the Brown family. He had secured [a] Hertz franchise for Lou [Nicole's father], he steered clients to Juditha's [Nicole's mother] travel business, and at one time or another he'd paid college tuition for two sisters and had given money to a third. He referred to this as Simpson's "largesse" [liberal giving].

Cochran declared Simpson to be incapable—both morally and physically—of the kind of violence displayed in the slayings of Nicole and Ron Goldman. He displayed photographs of Simpson clad only in blue bikini briefs to reveal the delimiting effects of old football injuries. And he called Simpson to the jury box to affirm the injuries. Judge Ito then denied Simpson's request to speak directly to the jury but allowed him to show the jurors the scars on his knees from several surgeries in the 1970s.

A Risky Strategy

At that point, Cochran hinted at an alternative defense strategy, suggesting that the murders of Nicole and Ron Goldman might be drug related. Faye Resnick, a close friend of Nicole's, had published a revealing book the previous summer, entitled *Nicole Brown Simpson: The Private Diary of a Life Interrupted*. In the book, Resnick stated flatly her belief in Simpson's guilt. She also disclosed a personal history of cocaine abuse. Because Resnick had been an occasional houseguest of Nicole's, Cochran then tried to link Resnick's drug abuse with a potential murder motive.

Longtime friend of Nicole, Faye Resnick, during testimony in the pre-trial. Resnick testified that O.J. was physically and verbally abusive. The defense tried to claim that Resnick was involved in a drug ring.

In a further indication of the defense's intent to keep its options open, Cochran charged that LAPD investigator Mark Fuhrman had once expressed racist opinions and may have planted the glove at Simpson's house. He further suggested that Detective Philip Vannatter may have sprinkled blood on Simpson's socks, implying that a police conspiracy to frame Simpson was entirely possible.

Cochran spoke for three hours. "For all the prosecution's seemingly damning points, Cochran offered counterpoints, many of them news to every listener," wrote *Time* correspondents Elaine Lafferty and James Willwerth. "But it was a strategy not without risk. Cochran must now deliver the credible witnesses and solid blood evidence that he promised."

A Rhetorical Question

On January 25, prosecutor William Hodgman reacted angrily to Cochran's assertions and to the defense's failure to disclose its witness list in a timely manner. That night, at a late meeting of the prosecution team, Hodgman suffered chest pains and was rushed to the hospital. His malady was diagnosed as a stress-related problem rather than a heart attack. He was released after two days but thereafter assumed a low-profile advisory role in the trial. Darden took over Hodgman's role as co-lead prosecutor with Marcia Clark.

After opening statements from both sides, Erwin Chemerinsky, a law professor at the University of Southern California, wrote: "After the prosecution finished, it seemed so clear that O.J. was guilty. Then after the defense finished, you felt he was not guilty. What more could you ask for?" Prosecutors hoped to answer Chemerinsky's rhetorical question with a conviction.

The Right Choices

On January 31, following a delay of two court days to argue procedural violations, the prosecution began its case. They called three witnesses to testify about the spousal abuse incident at Simpson's mansion on New Year's Day in 1989. Sharyn Gilbert, the 911 operator who took the call, and Mike Farrell and John

Edwards, two of the investigating officers, described the event.

From the beginning, prosecutors were concerned about being able to present a host of witnesses and a wealth of information in a timely fashion. Deputy District Attorney Scott Gordon, the D.A.'s specialist on domestic violence, explained: "Whenever you have a long trial, one that is so blocked, almost with separate trials on separate areas, it is hard to weave things together. . . . There was so much evidence, we had to make choices." Journalist Tom Elias wrote, "So for the sake of shortening the trial, prosecutors forsook some of the most compelling details of the Simpsons' often sordid life together." For instance, evidence that O.J. stalked his wife was never put before the jury. "Time," declared Elias, "was the only reason for this glaring omission."

The testimony of several more witnesses supported the prosecution's contention that spousal abuse often leads to murder. Prosecutors could only hope that they had made the right choices.

"A Dream Is a Wish Your Heart Makes"

Ron Shipp, a former Los Angeles police officer and close friend of Simpson's, shocked the court when he testified about a conversation he had with O.J. on the night after the murders. Shipp said that Simpson told him he felt reluctant to take a lie detector test because, "I *have* had some dreams about killing her."

Defense attorney Carl Douglas tried to discredit Shipp's testimony, portraying him as a liar and a drunk and accusing him of testifying to enhance his aspirations of becoming an actor. But Shipp did not flinch in the face of Douglas's taunts. Sheila Weller recalled:

> Carl Douglas's cross-examination of him was vicious. No commentator failed to remark on its venom. Yet, through it, Ron made the angry, spontaneous remarks that were so eloquent and riveting: "Mr. Douglas, I could care less about an acting career! Do you think I would put my family through this for an acting career? I'm doing this

for my conscience; I will not have the blood of Nicole on Ron Shipp; I can sleep at night, unlike a lot of others"; and, looking directly at O.J., the sorrowfully contemptuous; "This is sad, O.J. This is sad."

Then Marcia Clark added a deft counter of her own to Douglas's cross-examination of Shipp with a line straight out of Hollywood. "A dream is a wish your heart makes," she said.

A Sister's Story

On February 3, the prosecution continued its effort to show Simpson as a wife beater and abuser. Denise Brown, Nicole's look-alike sister, took the stand and related how Simpson publicly humiliated Nicole and how he once slammed her against the wall of their home. Denise told of a time when she and her boyfriend dined and drank with Simpson and Nicole in a Mexican restaurant. Afterward, the two couples retired to Simpson's estate and resumed drinking at his bar. Sobbing, Denise recalled:

Prosecutor Christopher Darden shows a photograph on the video screen of witness Ronald Shipp and O.J. Simpson while Shipp testifies on the witness stand.

I told him he took Nicole for granted, and he blew up. He started yelling—"Me? I don't take her for granted. I do everything for her. I give her everything."

And then a whole fight broke out. And pictures started flying off the walls. Clothes started flying. He ran upstairs, got clothes—started flying down the stairs, and um, grabbed Nicole, told her to get out of his house, wanted us all out of his house, picked her up, threw her against a wall.

Denise paused. Tears streamed down her face. She fingered a cross once belonging to Nicole and struggled to choke out the rest of her story.

[He] picked [Nicole] up, threw her out of the house, she ended up on her—she ended up falling, she ended up on her elbows and on her butt. Then he threw Ed McCabe [an executive who once dated Denise] out. We were all sitting there screaming and crying and he grabbed me and threw me out of the house.

Denise Brown breaks down in tears during testimony before the jury. Brown testified to O.J.'s abuse of Nicole.

The jurors sat fixed by Denise's testimony. A few glanced over at Simpson. Marcia Clark put her arm around a sobbing Denise and escorted her from the witness stand to end the court session.

The "Real O.J."

Denise concluded her testimony on the following Monday, February 6. Candace Garvey, wife of former baseball star Steve Garvey and friend of Nicole's, testified next about Simpson's behavior at his daughter Sydney's dance recital. Faye Resnick later recalled a conversation with Candace and Steve about O.J.'s demeanor:

> In the wake of the murders, I read press reports of people who'd seen O.J. that weekend—at a dinner party the night before and at other places. They said things like "he was in a fine mood," or "he sure didn't look like a guy who was going to kill his wife." I spoke to Candace and Steve Garvey about that final day. Their children had also been at the dance recital. They knew the real O.J., the man with the public happy, smiling face—and the private face that insiders sometimes see. Candace told me, "He was so despondent, in such a strange state of mind. I've never seen O.J. that way, ever!"

Candace Garvey described Simpson's behavior similarly in court.

Cynthia Shahian, jogging partner and friend of Nicole's, followed Candace to the stand. She told of a letter Simpson sent to Nicole in June regarding the Internal Revenue Service and of how frightened and upset Nicole became because of it. The letter implied that Simpson might report Nicole for declaring her home residence as the Rockingham location while she was actually living at the Bundy condo, a home she was supposed to be leasing out. In effect, Simpson was forcing Nicole to find another place to live or to immediately pay ninety thousand dollars to the IRS.

Faye Resnick tried at the time to persuade Simpson to reconsider such an action for the sake of the children. "Why go to such extremes?" she asked him. She wrote that he began ranting and screaming:

> You know why, Faye. It's because she doesn't want to be with me anymore. And I just can't be her friend anymore. I want her to be in as much pain as possible. Without me, she's nothing. Let her live in reality for a while so she'll appreciate how good she had it with me.

Shahian's testimony concluded, with unexpected suddenness, the prosecution's attack on Simpson's character.

The Timeline

On February 7, Judge Ito dismissed juror Katherine Murdoch, the third of ten jurors to be excused by trial's end. The prosecution then attempted to establish a timeline that would show a window of opportunity that afforded Simpson ample time to murder his wife and her friend.

Stewart Tanner, a bartender at Mezzaluna restaurant—where Ron Goldman worked and Nicole dined with family and friends on the night of the murders—testified about Goldman's last known activities. Nicole's neighbor, Pablo Fenjves, told the jury that he heard the "plaintive wail" of a dog between 10:15 and 10:20 P.M. on the night of the killings. Kimberly Goldman, Ron Goldman's sister, testified just long enough to identify work clothing found in her brother's apartment after his death. Tia Gavin and Karen Crawford, Mezzaluna employees, testified next to describe the last time they saw Ron Goldman, at about 9:45 P.M.

The following day five of Nicole's neighbors testified about the night of the murders. Eva Stein said the "very loud, very persistent" sound of a dog's barking awakened her at 10:15 P.M. Louis Karpf, Stein's fiancé, testified that he was outside getting his mail at 11:00 P.M., after returning from a trip, and "saw a dog [Nicole's dog Kato] in the street coming at me, barking very profusely. It started to approach me, which did scare me, so I actually retreated back inside my gate until it moved on."

Stephen Schwab described a large dog with bloody paws that he encountered outside a condominium while walking his own dog

RON GOLDMAN: THE KIND OF GUY HE WAS

"The only real hero in the case of *The People v. O.J. Simpson*, Ronald Goldman was a waiter and an aspiring actor who was killed trying to save the life of Nicole Brown," wrote Deputy District Attorney Christopher Darden.

Police can only speculate as to the precise sequence of events on the evening of June 12, 1994. But the evidence suggests that the twenty-six-year-old Goldman . . . fought hard and courageously against his assailant. That's the kind of guy he was.

"Outgoing and cocky. Adventurous, yet relaxed. This, in his own words, was Ronald Goldman." So wrote AP correspondent Linda Deutsch. In a terse, revealing profile of Goldman, shown here in part, she went on to write:

> He was more than just a waiter. More than Nicole Brown Simpson's friend. More than just a name in a headline. . . .
>
> "He was always having fun," says longtime friend Mike Pincus. "He lived day-to-day." . . . After dropping out of college, Goldman lived with his family in suburban Agoura Hills and held a string of jobs waiting tables, hoping to gain enough experience so he could open his own restaurant, said his father, Fred Goldman.
>
> "That's why he had jobs at restaurants. He was getting a handle on what it took," his father said. "He was putting his life back together.". . . The suburban life soon proved too inhibiting, and Goldman set his sights on Brentwood, a fashionable Westside area where he could hobnob with the rich and famous. . . .
>
> In Brentwood, Goldman found himself surrounded by a clique of well-toned, youthful bodies who hung out at a Starbucks coffee shop that sits on a bustling boulevard, across from the Mezzaluna restaurant where Goldman worked and Nicole Brown Simpson often dined. . . .
>
> It was at Starbucks, friends say, where Goldman and Ms. Simpson first met, several months before their lives came to a savage end on the pathway of her condo. . . .
>
> The friendship ultimately cost Goldman his life when he offered to return a pair of glasses Ms. Simpson's mother had left at Mezzaluna, where her family had dined that night. It was an errand his friends say was entirely in character.
>
> "He would open his heart to anyone," Pincus says. "You'd ask him for a favor and he would do it."

Darden was right. The only "real hero" in the Simpson case was Ron Goldman. He died helping a friend . . . because that's the kind of guy he was.

at 10:55 P.M. The dog followed him home, he said, and "would howl at every house we passed. It would stop and bark down the path."

Sukru Boztepe testified how he and his wife were led to the crime scene by the Akita dog (Kato) and found Nicole's body. "I saw a lady laying down, full of blood," he told the jury. "She was blonde. I could see her arm."

And Elsie Tistaert, an elderly woman who lived nearby, attested to hearing a dog barking for a half hour and calling 911 at midnight when she thought she heard prowlers.

Piecing together the testimony of a string of witnesses, the prosecution established a workable timeline. "The timing of the crime is critical," wrote Linda Deutsch. "Prosecutors allege[d] Simpson killed his ex-wife and Goldman at 10:15 P.M., allowing himself enough time to return to his estate, clean up and get into a limousine for the airport at about 11:00 P.M." Deutsch added that defense attorney Johnnie Cochran "ridiculed the prosecution's effort to convict Simpson based on a dog's howl."

"The Critical Point in the Trial"

Marcia Clark showed gory crime-scene photographs, with LAPD officer Robert Riske on the stand to describe their lurid details. Mr. and Mrs. Brown, Nicole's parents, left the courtroom before the photos were shown, but Mrs. Goldman and Kimberly remained seated. Kim wept softly.

On Sunday, February 12, the jurors visited the Bundy crime scene and Brentwood area on an official jury tour. Robert Shapiro reported that while at the Rockingham location Simpson scoffed, "Who would give all this up? Who would jeopardize this kind of life, this kind of family?" His questions may never be answered.

Officer Riske returned to the stand on February 14, followed by LAPD sergeant David Rossi. Cochran cross-examined Riske; F. Lee Bailey, in his first active appearance, cross-examined Rossi. The officers described what occurred at Bundy Drive after their arrival. Homicide detectives Ronald Phillips and Tom Lange appeared next to testify about going to Simpson's estate and what happened there.

Defense lawyers, as they would throughout the trial, tried to elicit testimony indicative of police bungling and mishandling of evidence. Christopher Darden later expressed his disgust with Johnnie Cochran's cross-examination of Riske, Judge Lance Ito's forbearance, and the timidity of police witnesses in general:

> [Cochran's] cross[-examination] had been long-winded and beside the point, asking Riske questions that he knew—and Judge Ito should have known—weren't relevant for a patrol officer with no homicide training. It was like putting a high school science teacher on the stand and grilling him about nuclear fission reactors to show how ill-trained he was. Cochran's voice dripped with sarcasm and condescension. The end result was that officers like Riske were on the stand for five or six days, carefully answering questions they should have just dismissed.

> Just once I wished one of the cops would roll his eyes and say, "That's the dumbest question I've ever heard." But the defense team had the LAPD so uptight, they marched in like lambs to slaughter. I couldn't believe it. These were tough, capable cops. Why were they letting the defense do this?

O.J. and lawyers during the jury tour of the crime scene. The jury toured the scene of the crime and Simpson's estate to try to determine whether Simpson could have driven from one to the other using the prosecution's timeline.

Judge Ito replaced a fourth juror, Michael Knox, for "just cause," as the trial moved into March. Now came the critical point in the trial," wrote Darden. "From Riske to the crime lab workers to the lead detectives, Tom Lange and Phil Vannatter, all defense roads led through Mark Fuhrman."

All Was Not as It Seemed

Detective Mark Fuhrman took the stand on March 9. Fuhrman, accused of being a racist by the defense and destined to become the trial's most critical witness, told Marcia Clark about the police investigation at Bundy Drive and at Rockingham, including his discovery of the bloody glove.

During his cross-examination of Detective Fuhrman, F. Lee Bailey introduced the *n* word into the trial. "Do you use the word 'nigger' in describing people?" Bailey asked.

"No, sir."

"Have you used that word in the past ten years?"

"Not that I recall," Fuhrman replied.

Bailey rephrased the question several times and eventually asked, "And you say under oath that you have not addressed any black person as 'nigger' or spoken about black people as niggers in the past ten years, Detective Fuhrman?"

"That's what I'm saying, sir."

An article in *People* magazine quoted Fuhrman as saying, "This is not a racial issue. This is about a guy that murdered someone. And he was sloppy. I did my job. It irritates the defense the most because I did it right." Or so it then seemed.

Chapter 4

Creating a
Reasonable Doubt

L EAD LAPD DETECTIVE PHILIP VANNATTER followed Detective Mark Fuhrman to the stand on March 16. Vannatter, a twenty-five-year veteran of the LAPD, testified that it was his decision to send Fuhrman over the wall at Rockingham. He gave a detailed account of how the police analyzed the situation and gathered evidence at the crime scene.

After court that day, defense counsel Robert Shapiro shocked reporters outside the Criminal Courts Building by announcing that he disagreed with others of the defense team over the race issue. Race, he felt, should not be an issue in the case. His colleagues hastened to assure the press that there was no split in the ranks of the Dream Team. But rumors of their dissension persisted.

"The Way the System Works"

Shapiro cross-examined Vannatter the following week and called attention to some alleged breaches of investigative procedures. "Phil Vannatter was a seasoned detective as well as a shrewd, cagey, experienced witness," Shapiro wrote later. "He liked to look jurors in the eye, to make a connection with them while he proved that he knew what he was doing." Shapiro recalled:

> I had no bombs to drop on Vannatter, no sweeping moment of impeachment. Just a few, simple questions, which he could not and did not answer to my satisfaction.

67

Why was so much time spent at Rockingham, at the expense of the Bundy crime scene? Was there a rush to judgment, a decision in the early hours of June 13 that O.J. Simpson was absolutely, positively, irrefutably the murderer? And why, when O.J. Simpson's blood was drawn minutes away from the police laboratory on June 13, did Vannatter then carry it in his pocket for three hours?

Shapiro contrasted Vannatter's demeanor with that of Detective Tom Lange, whose disposition the lawyer described as "stoic and whose answers had been direct." Shapiro portrayed Vannatter as

the kind of old-school cop who was too impatient to go by the book, who believed even as he shaded the truth that the end justified the means. He wasn't beyond adjusting or tailoring his testimony to make evidence, and his behavior, look better than it actually was, and I had to get the jury to see that.

Afterward, wrote Shapiro, his wife, Linell, criticized his handling of Vannatter's cross-examination:

Police detective Philip Vannatter points to his finger during testimony, showing where Simpson's finger had been cut. The cut on Simpson's hand matched the hole in the bloody glove.

He was a decent, hard-working cop, she said, whom I'd made to look much worse than he was. Maybe he was an old-school cop who bent the rules now and then. Maybe he was a little loose with the truth. But he was hardly in the same league as Fuhrman.

"As for Tom Lange, I always figured that he didn't take it personally," Shapiro concluded. "We both had our jobs to do, and like me, Lange had been around long enough to know that that's the way the system works."

The Natural

On March 21, the prosecution called on Brian "Kato" Kaelin, by then the world's most famous houseguest, to testify about the defendant's demeanor and whereabouts on the night of the murders. Marcia Clark asked Kaelin, an aspiring actor, whether he thought of Simpson as someone who could help his acting career. His answer inspired a round of laughter in the usually staid courtroom. "I didn't think we were going for the same parts," he said. Kaelin's testimony added a little humor to the proceedings, and an equal amount of support for the prosecution's timeline.

Co-prosecutor Christopher Darden reported later on Kaelin's testimony and its value to the people's case:

> Kato said he'd gone to get a hamburger with Simpson about 9 P.M. [June 12, 1994], and an hour after returning from McDonald's, he'd heard three loud thumps outside Simpson's house [guest quarters] in the walkway where the bloody glove was later found. That hour in between—during which Simpson was unaccounted for—was when Nicole Brown and Ronald Goldman were murdered.

Darden thought it strange that Simpson had made several phone calls to Kaelin on the day after the killings, since O.J. and Kato were not that close.

> But the reason became apparent when one of Kaelin's friends told us that Simpson had said to Kaelin, "Thank God, you can tell them I was home all the time." O.J. was fishing for an alibi.

Kato Kaelin, former unemployed actor and full-time houseguest of Simpson. Kato's bizarre way of communicating spawned the term "Kato-speak."

Kato wasn't willing to go that far for Simpson, but he wasn't much help to investigators either. At first, in the days following the murders, he was coy, refusing to answer questions. We received tips that he'd told friends that he had crucial information. By the time he testified, in late March, he was as helpful as a pile of hair.

As Darden continued, he made scant effort to conceal his contempt:

I've rarely seen a witness work so hard to be vague and inconclusive on the stand. He denied that Simpson had asked him to be his alibi. Kato later recalled Simpson as being animated and upset about Nicole, even though, on the stand, he said Simpson didn't seem particularly angry the night of the murders. Only after treating him as a hostile witness did Marcia finally get Kaelin to admit—in Kato-speak—that "there was some upsetness."

"Throughout his testimony," Darden summarized, "Kato played dumb. It was the perfect role for him; he was a natural."

A TIMELINE AND TWO KATOS

"Witnesses like Kato Kaelin and Allan Park showed that Simpson wasn't home during the time in which his wife was killed and that he had no explanation for a seventy-eight-minute gap and no alibi," wrote prosecutor Christopher Darden in his book *In Contempt*. "He had motive; he had opportunity."

The seventy-eight-minute gap referred to by Darden commenced on June 12, 1994, at 9:36 P.M. It ended at 10:54 P.M. According to the prosecution's theory, the murders of Nicole Brown Simpson and Ronald Goldman occurred at approximately 10:15 that evening. A timeline—as shown in *Verdict: The Chronicle of the O.J. Simpson Trial*, by AP correspondents Linda Deutsch and Michael Fleeman—shows what prosecutors believed to be Simpson's window of opportunity for committing the murders:

> **9:10 P.M.:** Simpson drives houseguest Brian "Kato" Kaelin to McDonald's in his Bentley.
>
> **9:36 P.M.:** Simpson and Kaelin return to Simpson's estate on Rockingham Avenue.
>
> **10:03 P.M.:** Simpson telephones his girlfriend, Paula Barbieri, from the cellular telephone in his Bronco.
>
> **10:15 P.M.:** Nicole Simpson's neighbor Pablo Fenjves hears a dog barking, then a "plaintive wail."
>
> **10:22 P.M.:** Limousine driver Allan Park drives down Rockingham and doesn't see Bronco.
>
> **10:40 P.M.:** Park pulls up to the gate on Ashford Street and rings the buzzer. Nobody answers.
>
> **10:45–50 P.M.:** Ms. Simpson's neighbor sees Ms. Simpson's Akita, with bloody paws, on the sidewalk outside her house.
>
> **10:51–52 P.M.:** Kaelin hears three thumps on the wall outside his guest house.
>
> **10:54 P.M.:** Park sees a man he believes is Simpson entering the front door at Rockingham.
>
> **11:15 P.M.:** Simpson and Park leave for the airport.

Attorney Alan Dershowitz, in his book *Reasonable Doubts*, later gave voice to the defense's view of the critical timeline. "The defense made a powerful showing that Simpson could not have committed two brutal and bloody murders, cleaned himself up, and gotten back home in the time between the wails of the dog and the three bangs on the air conditioner," he wrote. "In any event, to the extent that the prosecution was relying on the 'testimony' of the two Katos—the dog who wailed and the houseguest who heard the three bangs—it was not operating from strength."

The Celebrity Appears

On March 29, limousine driver Allan Park, who had chauffeured Simpson to the airport on the night of the murders, added further support for the timeline. Park testified that he arrived at the Rockingham address twenty minutes early and did not see Simpson's Bronco for seventeen minutes. Journalist Dennis Schatzman wrote:

> He had an order to pick up Simpson at 10:45 P.M. on Sunday, June 12. Park said he arrived early about 10:25 P.M. and parked at the corner of Rockingham and Ashford, across from Simpson's estate. He said he never saw or "noticed" if there was a white Ford Bronco at the side of the house.
>
> After smoking a cigarette, Park said he pulled up to the gate at 10:40 P.M. and began ringing the intercom. . . . "I rang the intercom," Park told the court. "And there was no answer." He said he noticed that one light was on upstairs. None on downstairs. He called his boss at 10:50 P.M. "Mr. Simpson is always running late," Park says his boss told him. "Just wait until 11:15 P.M."

Limousine driver Allan Park, left, testifies while Johnnie Cochran displays a piece of luggage during the murder trial.

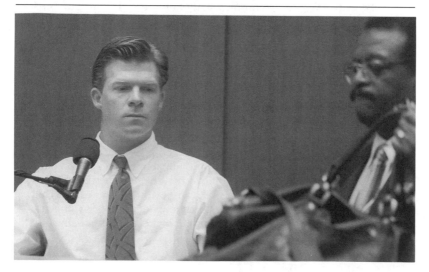

Park testified that he then saw a white male (Kato Kaelin) emerge from behind the Ashford side of the house. Schatzman went on with Park's testimony:

> "Almost simultaneously, when I saw him, I saw someone black cross the driveway and go into the house." The person was over six feet tall and weighed over 200 pounds, Park said. "I couldn't tell who it was, whether it was a male or a female."

> Park rang the buzzer again, and this time "I got an answer from a person who I believed was Mr. Simpson. He told me that he had overslept and that he just got out of the shower and he'd be down in a few minutes."

Commenting on Park's testimony, AP correspondent Linda Deutsch pointed out that only after Park saw a large black figure enter the house did Simpson answer the intercom. "And within six minutes he was on the doorstep with his bags," she wrote, "appearing every inch the celebrity dressed for the spotlight." Simpson and Park departed for the airport at 11:15 P.M.

The Battle of the Experts

On March 27, the prosecution shifted into a new phase that could well be entitled "the battle of the experts." Autopsy photographs of Nicole and Ron Goldman—huge pictures projected on a seven-foot screen—were shown and analyzed by the prosecutors and expert witnesses, ostensibly to refute defense claims that two people committed the murders. Los Angeles County coroner Dr. Lakshmanan Sathyavagiswaran testified about the victims' wounds and demonstrated how one person could have killed both Nicole and Ron. The Associated Press diagrammed the prosecution's murder theory in four steps, as follows:

> 1. The assailant stabs Nicole Simpson four times in the neck. At about the same time, she also has her head smashed against a gate or metal post.

> 2. The killer restrains Ronald Goldman with his left hand and carefully makes parallel cuts across his neck.

Later, the assailant stabs Goldman behind the left ear and in the heart and lung.

3. With Goldman dead or dying, the attacker returns to Ms. Simpson, who may be unconscious, and pulls her head back by the hair. He slashes her throat with a knife in his right hand, killing her almost instantly.

4. The killer runs [or walks] away up the steps to the back alley of Ms. Simpson's condo.

The grisly autopsy photographs remained on display all that day. Beyond affirming its one-murderer theory, the prosecution may have entertained a less obvious motive for keeping them before the jury throughout the day-long session. Peter Arenella, professor of law at UCLA, afterward pointed out:

> In a trial in which the victims are gone but the defendant is in front of the jury every day, it's easier for the jury to relate to his humanity. The prosecution wants a constant reminder of the victim's humanity and the pictures provide that.

Coroner Lakshmanan Sathyavagiswaran gestures to his neck as he testifies about Nicole's injuries. Although Sathyavagiswaran testified that there was only one killer, under cross-examination he admitted that he could not be sure.

Simpson looks skyward during the coroner's testimony about Nicole's wounds.

Arenella might have added, as well, that the pictures also served as a reminder of the *in*humanity of the killer or killers. And there was more evidence of such yet to be revealed in the battle of the experts.

"The Great Serological Snooze"

In a murder case without an eyewitness, the prosecution must rely on the weight and quality of circumstantial evidence to prove its case beyond a reasonable doubt. Prosecutors expected that the weight of DNA blood evidence would tip the scales of justice in their direction.

On May 10, Dr. Robin Cotton, director of laboratories for Cellmark Diagnostics (where most of the DNA analysis was done), began DNA blood analysis testimony. Of her testimony, Dominick Dunne, veteran courtroom reporter and author, wrote:

> According to Cotton, the blood found near the victims could have come from only 1 person in 170 million African-Americans and Caucasians. That blood matched O.J. Simpson's blood. The blood on the sock in Simpson's

bedroom was consistent with that of only 1 person out of 6.8 billion—more people than there are on earth—and that blood matched the blood of Nicole Brown Simpson.

Defense attorney Johnnie Cochran said he didn't think Cotton's testimony was "damaging at all." But the prosecution backed up Cotton's findings with those of a second, independent source. Prosecutor Christopher Darden wrote:

> After Cotton, we called Gary Sims, of the California Department of Justice, which had done DNA tests independent of Cellmark and had come to the same conclusions. When these two witnesses were done, we had presented a trail of evidence as conclusive as a videotape of Simpson committing the murders. More conclusive, in fact. It would have been more likely for a person who looked exactly like Simpson to show up on videotape than for the blood to have been from someone else.

"During [Barry] Scheck's cross[-examination] of Sims," recounted Robert Shapiro, "the witness couldn't immediately locate one piece of information in his notes." Shapiro then illustrated Scheck's competence:

> Scheck had the data in front of him. Scheck said, "Well, would you agree if I told you that . . . ?" and then recited the data. Responded Sims, "Mr. Scheck, I'll take your word for anything."

Both men were clear speakers; they knew this was a tough audience. But the testimony was dense, confusing, and the jurors were obviously bored. Scheck raised the possibility that someone not identified in the case left blood at the scene, but there was no way of knowing if the jury picked up on this. . . .

Scheck was impressive, both in his knowledge of the science and the dogged way he cross-examined a witness until he got what he wanted.

THE WORTH AND PROMISE OF DNA TESTING

On May 28, 1995, at the height of the prosecution's presentation of DNA evidence in the O.J. Simpson trial, the *New York Times* published the following evocative editorial, entitled "The Power of DNA Evidence":

> The most important development in recent weeks may be the respect accorded to the science of DNA blood testing. Even in this bitterly contested murder trial, the principles and potential of DNA testing have not yet been seriously questioned. Indeed, the defense has not generally challenged the validity of the science but has instead charged that the blood evidence was mishandled or manipulated by conspiratorial police before it was subjected to DNA analysis.

> Although DNA analysis is on display as never before, its worth and promise have been apparent for a decade in thousands of cases. Scientists, lawyers and judges find that the technology can often clear—or incriminate—a suspect in crimes or paternity cases. This is a valuable identification tool, especially because eyewitness identification is often very shaky.

> Far less evident, at least at this stage of a long and dreary trial, is whether the science can be clear or convincing to a jury of non-scientists. Do these jurors actually absorb the crash course in genetics and rightly interpret those blurry X-ray pictures of little blobs that the criminalists tell them are matching blood samples? How many among the millions watching on television can honestly say they understand the evidence?

> Even knowledgeable observers may rebel at the spiraling claims of numerical accuracy. Few people know how to evaluate prosecution contentions that there is only a 1-in-170-million chance that someone other than Mr. Simpson matched a particular blood spot on the walkway where his [ex-]wife, Nicole, and her friend Ron Goldman were knifed to death. As for Mr. Simpson's bloody sock, only one in nearly seven billion people supposedly match Nicole Simpson's blood type found there, so a search of the planet might not turn up another match. Is it possible that jurors will find the numbers numbing and the experts tyrannical, and then devise their own formula for determining whether a reasonable doubt exists? . . .

> With DNA testing becoming more readily available, judges and juries may become increasingly dependent on it and create a greater demand for its use. Both sides will be impelled to use it or be subtly pressured to explain not using it. With both legal teams engaged in a common pursuit of DNA evidence, trials might become more of a "search for truth" on some issues than is typically the case.

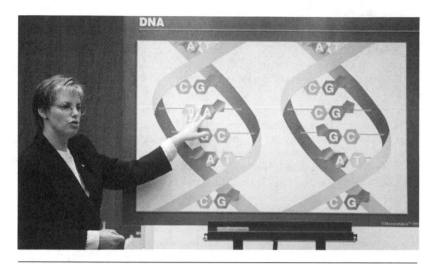

Robin Cotton, director of Cellmark Labs, explains DNA to the jury. Many argue that Cotton's testimony was overly complex for the jury—only one of whom had a college education.

The trial dragged on as prosecution witnesses took jurors on a tour of DNA testing techniques, and the defense tried doggedly to discredit the prosecution's test methods and handling of blood evidence. Their protracted claims and counterclaims inspired *U.S. News & World Report* correspondent Betsy Streisand to call that phase of the trial "the Great Serological Snooze."

The Turning Point

By June 5, ten jurors had been replaced. On June 15, in what likely will be remembered always as the trial's turning point, Christopher Darden asked Simpson to try on the bloody gloves found at Bundy and beside Simpson's Brentwood guest quarters.

Darden felt that such a demonstration would inextricably link Simpson with the murders in the minds of the jurors. Simpson obliged in full view of the jury. After donning latex gloves, he struggled to pull the bloody gloves over them.

"They're too small," Simpson said. To the everlasting embarrassment and dismay of the prosecution in general—and to Christopher Darden in particular—*the gloves didn't fit*. Or so it seemed. Darden thought otherwise:

He was [faking] and I hoped everyone could see that, hoped the jury could see it. But as I glanced quickly around the courtroom, I saw that everyone else was staring at his hands and not his face.

At first, his eyebrows were arched and his mouth set, nervous, like someone about to dive off a bridge. Then he broke into a weird, relieved smile, unlike any I'd seen in any of the old football footage or any of his movies, a smile that I think was as close to the real O.J. Simpson as I'd ever seen, as if he'd surprised even himself.

My God, I'm getting away with it.

He gestured at me, as if to ask if I wanted to try to push the gloves onto his hands, then he showed the gloves proudly to the jury, whose members scribbled furiously. "Mr. Simpson is indicating that his fingers aren't all the way into the gloves, your honor," I said. "Can we ask him to straighten his fingers and extend them into the glove as one might normally put a glove on?"

In one of the most famous blunders of the trial, Simpson tries on the bloody glove, claiming that it does not fit. The moment would spawn Cochran's line, "If it doesn't fit, you must acquit."

The courtroom swirled around me, wide-eyed faces staring, the room falling away. I said flatly, "Mr. Simpson told the jury that the gloves are too small."

In the minds of most legal analysts—and perhaps untold millions of TV viewers around the world—that moment became the turning point of the O.J. Simpson trial.

An Unceremonious Ending

The prosecution ended its case on July 6. The next day, in the *New York Times*, journalist David Margolick wrote:

> LOS ANGELES, July 6—With some final fragments of hair and fiber evidence and a statement from Nicole Brown Simpson's mother, prosecutors at the O.J. Simpson trial quietly and unceremoniously rested this afternoon—92 days of testimony, 58 witnesses, 488 exhibits, and 34,500 transcript pages after they began.

Opinions of the prosecution's case from trial observers quoted by Margolick differed. LAPD detective Tom Lange said, "The physical evidence, the condition it was found under—it places him [Simpson] everywhere at the right time."

Lead defense counsel Johnnie Cochran opined, "I thought they tried the best they could under the circumstances [but] I think we made a lot of points on their case." Now the time had arrived for Cochran and the Dream Team to make points on their own case.

Los Angeles defense lawyer Harlan Braun said, "Hopefully this case survived the prosecution. They basically took a case that was overwhelming and created a reasonable doubt."

Chapter 5

Lingering Echoes
of Racism

T HE DEFENSE BEGAN ITS CASE on July 10. "From here on, the defense strategy was to present credible demeanor witnesses to undo the prosecution's 'demonization' of O.J. and timeline witnesses to refute the prosecution's theory of when the murders took place," wrote defense attorney Robert Shapiro. "Drs. [Michael] Baden and [Henry] Lee would then further

Cochran, Shapiro, and Simpson. Simpson's lawyers would attempt to portray him as a man incapable of the kind of violence exacted upon Nicole and Ron Goldman.

counter the prosecution's forensic witnesses, arguing that errors in procedure and judgment had created a scenario that was possible but not provable."

Demeanor Witnesses

"One of the most important factors in a defense case is the demeanor of the defendant around the time of the crime," continued Shapiro. "How did he look? How did he behave? Witnesses who can testify to these questions from their firsthand knowledge are called 'demeanor witnesses.'"

The defense called Simpson's older daughter, Arnelle, as their first witness, followed by sisters Shirley Baker and Carmelita Simpson Durio, and mother, Eunice. They filled the courtroom with warm recollections of family memories aimed at portraying Simpson as a kind and loving father, brother, and son. Of Arnelle, Shapiro wrote:

> A beautiful and charming young woman, she radiated the love and trust she had for her father, and he beamed

Simpson's daughter Arnelle testified that Simpson was a loving, devoted father.

across the room at her as she testified. She spoke very movingly about his shock and sadness at Nicole's death. She was a perfect, unimpeachable witness. The prosecution knew that and left her alone on cross-examination.

Arnelle drew a smile from Simpson when she said, "I was born the same day my dad won the Heisman Trophy."

The fragile seventy-three-year-old Eunice had to be helped out of her wheelchair and then hobbled with much difficulty to the witness stand. She spoke hesitatingly about the family's history and the difficulties of raising four children as a divorced mother. Asked how the family reacted to news of the murders on the evening of June 13, she said, "We were gripping each other." And what of Ron Shipp's demeanor that night? "He appeared to be spaced," she said of the ex-cop who had been sitting at the bar drinking beer. Her comment drew a murmur from the spectators.

Additional so-called demeanor witnesses for the defense included airline pilot Wayne Stanfield, who flew the plane Simpson took to Chicago on the night of the killings, and Mark Partridge, an attorney and fellow passenger on Simpson's return flight to Los Angeles the next day.

Stanfield testified that at 2:45 A.M. he approached Simpson for an autograph at thirty-one thousand feet. Mr. Simpson, he said, was staring out the window at the time, pensively "lost in thought." Partridge's testimony echoed what he had told a reporter earlier: "It was evident from the phone calls he was making and the comments he made during the flight that a great tragedy was affecting his life and the lives of his children. . . . I remember feeling very sorry for him."

Points for the Prosecution

On July 12, the prosecution scored a point of its own through the testimony of defense timeline witness Robert Heidstra, a neighbor of Nicole's who routinely walked his aged, arthritic dogs about 10:30 in the evening. In an article for the *New York Times* the next day, reporter David Margolick wrote:

In direct examination, Mr. Heidstra said that he had seen [a] white vehicle, possibly a Blazer or Jeep Cherokee, pull up to the corner of Bundy and Dorothy at 10:40 P.M. Under cross-examination, Mr. Heidstra conceded that the vehicle could have been a Ford Bronco.

Christopher Darden scored again when Heidstra also conceded that a speeding car probably could travel from Bundy to Rockingham in four minutes. And had the witness seen the white vehicle stop suddenly and accelerate quickly? "Yes," Heidstra said, "it looks like that person's in a hurry."

The prosecution also benefited when Simpson's physician, Dr. Robert Huizenga, contradicted defense claims that Simpson was not physically capable of committing the murders. Huizenga, a Beverly Hills internist, testified that although the former football star was still on "significant anti-rheumatoid arthritis medication," Simpson was sufficiently able-bodied to have done the crime.

Dr. Robert Huizenga places his hand on an outline of Simpson's left hand during testimony. Huizenga supported the defense's theory that the cuts on Simpson's hand were probably made by glass rather than a knife.

"What Is on Those Tapes?"

Just after the Fourth of July weekend, defense investigator Bill Pavelic learned of the existence of audiotapes containing twelve hours of interviews between Detective Mark Fuhrman and would-be screenwriter Laura Hart McKinny. The tapes, part of McKinny's research for a screenplay about the LAPD, purportedly contained racial slurs voiced by Fuhrman.

"In the middle of July," wrote Robert Shapiro, "we informed Judge Ito of the existence and substance of Laura Hart McKinny's taped interviews with Mark Fuhrman." Shapiro went on:

> Based on the brief excerpts we'd heard and the information we'd given him, the judge agreed that they were material to the case and immediately issued a subpoena for their return to this jurisdiction.

> At the end of July, Johnnie Cochran went to North Carolina armed with the subpoena. There a local judge blocked our attempt to get McKinny's Fuhrman tapes, ruling that the tapes were only collateral, not material, to the question of O.J.'s guilt, and therefore the defense had no right to them.

> It was a major setback for us. Shocked and frustrated by the ruling, Cochran announced our intention to appeal. At this point the news was out. From one end of the country to the other we heard the question: What is on those tapes?

The North Carolina appellate court overruled the lower court ruling on August 7 and ordered that the tapes be delivered to the Simpson defense. While prosecutors wrangled unsuccessfully to take ownership of the controversial tapes, the country waited eagerly to learn what was on them.

A Second Medical Opinion

On August 10, the defense called on Dr. Michael Baden, co-director of the forensics unit of the New York State Police Department in Albany, to refute the prosecution's forensic evidence and single-killer contention. In opposition to the prosecution's theory that the killings of Nicole Brown Simpson and Ron Goldman took only about a minute each, Baden testified that the victims put up a long fight—as long as fifteen minutes—and that there is no way to determine how many killers were involved. Journalist David Margolick recapped Baden's testimony in the *New York Times* the next day:

> In testimony that was brisk, graphic and gruesome, leaving the victims' families and Mr. Simpson alike with eyes watering, Dr. Baden was much more protracted. Both victims were conscious, resisting and capable of screaming, taxing the skills and nimbleness of a sole strong perpetrator, the doctor said.

> And throughout his interrogation, Robert L. Shapiro, a defense lawyer, referred pointedly to "assailant" or "assailants."

> Contradicting the testimony of Dr. Sathyavagiswaran, who once worked under him at Bellevue Hospital in New York, Dr. Baden testified that Mrs. Simpson's head injury and the angle from which blood gushed from her carotid artery indicated she had not been knocked unconscious before she was killed. That unconsciousness, the coroner had testified, would have allowed Mr. Simpson to attack Mr. Goldman, carrying samples of Mrs. Simpson's hair with him, and then return to finish her off.

> Multiple defensive wounds throughout Mrs. Simpson's body suggested that she was a moving and persistent target, Dr. Baden said. "My opinion is that she struggled with the assailant or assailants prior to succumbing when her neck was cut," he said.

> As the doctor detailed the mauling that Mrs. Simpson suffered, Mr. Simpson took deep gulps of water, pursed his lips, sighed and nodded his head.

Mr. Goldman put up even more of a fight, Dr. Baden said, suffering 22 stab wounds or more on his face and neck, chest and abdomen "depending on how one counted." A cut on his right shoe indicated that he even kicked the assailant.

While blood gushed from Mrs. Simpson's carotid artery, the doctor said, blood only oozed from Mr. Goldman's jugular vein, leaving him as much as 15 minutes to stand and fight for his life.

Ron Goldman, the innocent victim who died because he was in the wrong place at the wrong time.

The court recessed for the morning. Dr. Baden continued his testimony that afternoon. As recapped by Margolick, Baden said:

> Mr. Goldman had injured his knuckle from hitting some- one, not while brushing against a tree or fence behind him. He theorized that a blow hard enough to harm Mr. Goldman would probably have been hard enough to leave a mark on his attacker. Mr. Simpson bore no such signs after the killings.

> Dr. Sathyavagiswaran has subscribed to the single-killer theory, speculating that the killer was probably larger than Mr. Goldman and used one single-edged knife. But Dr. Baden said no one could say how many killers were involved, their height and weight, or what weapon or weapons they used.

After quizzing Dr. Baden for three hours, attorney Shapiro yielded his witness to Deputy District Attorney Brian Kelberg. In an attempt to dilute the effects of Dr. Baden's testimony on the jury, Kelberg sprang to the attack. He suggested, Margolick reported, "that Dr. Baden was a publicity hound and a hired gun." "Dr. Baden," wrote the *Times* reporter, "conceded he had already received more than $100,000 for his services in the case."

Kelberg also tried to discredit the defense's explanation that Simpson had cut his finger on his cellular phone before leaving for Chicago—thus accounting for the blood drops found at his home—and had cut it again on a broken glass after his arrival in Chicago. But Dr. Baden countered many of Kelberg's queries with lengthy monologues on his medical career and accomplishments.

A Cruel and Unfair Ruling

Also that day Judge Lance A. Ito took possession of Laura Hart McKinny's audiotapes, which threatened to impeach Detective Mark Fuhrman and his key testimony for the prosecution. Three days later Marcia Clark informed Judge Ito that she would ask him to remove himself from the trial. She cited an apparent conflict of interest stemming from derogatory comments made by Fuhrman on the tapes about Ito's police-captain wife. (Fuhrman was also said to have made many racist and sexist remarks during the recorded interviews and to have spoken of LAPD officers lying and covering up for colleagues and fabricating evidence.) Clark withdrew her threat when superior court judge John Reid ruled that Ito's wife was not a relevant trial witness.

District Attorney Gil Garcetti, when questioned by the media about the damaging effects of the "Fuhrman Tapes" on the prosecution's key witness, tried to distance himself from Fuhrman:

Is he a key witness? I'd probably argue no. We have so much evidence, we have so many witnesses from all parts of our community, not just from law enforcement. I would argue quite forcefully and persuasively that even if you didn't have that glove [found by Fuhrman], you have a powerful, powerful case.

Laura McKinny opened a Pandora's box for the prosecution when she testified about Fuhrman's racism. Although McKinny's testimony had nothing to do with Simpson's relative guilt, she was able to impeach Fuhrman's credibility.

On August 16, in a closed session with Judge Ito, prosecutor Clark tried to allay the tapes' potentially devastating effect on her case and Fuhrman's credibility. She told the judge that during the taped interviews Fuhrman did "a lot of exaggerating for the purposes of a book of fiction."

Ito subsequently ruled that the jury could hear only two of forty-one tape excerpts in which Fuhrman referred to blacks as "niggers." After Ito ruled, lead defender Johnnie Cochran held a press conference. "To say we are outraged and livid by this ruling would be a master understatement," he told reporters. "Today, you saw perhaps one of the cruelest, unfair decisions ever rendered in a criminal court in this country."

"Something Is Wrong"

"Through July and August, the defense presented experts who argued that the evidence *could be interpreted* to show tampering or incompetence on the part of police," Christopher Darden noted. "As a lawyer you learn quickly that there are expert witnesses who will tailor their expertise to whatever a defense lawyer needs."

Dr. Henry Lee, an internationally renowned and respected forensic scientist and crime-scene expert, cannot be so grouped. Impeccably unbiased, Dr. Lee's background reflects a willingness to testify without prejudice for either the prosecution or the defense as to the integrity of forensic evidence.

Near the end of August, the personable Lee, speaking simply and directly in English, but in an accent heavily rooted in the rhythms of his Chinese heritage, captured and held the jurors' attention like no other witness. According to Robert Shapiro:

> The focus of Dr. Lee's testimony was to point out the errors in the district attorney's crime-scene reconstruction. Among these was Lee's identification of what he thought might be a shoeprint on Ron Goldman's jeans—a print that came not from a Bruno Magli shoe, he said, but possibly a second killer. This finding was not a definitive one, he was quick to say, it was only a possibility that had been overlooked by the coroner. . . .
>
> He challenged the integrity of some of the blood spots removed from the crime scene and testified about the swatches of blood samples he was allowed to examine in the L.A.P.D. lab. They were damp, he said. If they had been properly stored, they should have been dry by the time he looked at them. "Only opinion I can give under these circumstances—something wrong," he said.
>
> Like all good witnesses, he tried to reduce scientific testimony to a metaphor that the jury could readily grasp. He compared the lab contamination to finding a cockroach in a plate of spaghetti. "All you need is one . . . and you know it is contaminated."
>
> When [prosecutor] Hank Goldberg foolishly tried to challenge him, Dr. Lee again responded firmly, "Something is wrong."

After Dr. Lee's testimony and the discovery of the Fuhrman tapes, the focus of the trial shifted abruptly away from scientific evidence.

Forensic scientist and defense witness Henry Lee describes how blood stains were transferred from evidence items to paper bags by police investigators.

The Fuhrman Tapes

The high point of O.J. Simpson's defense came on September 5 with the introduction in court of the two taped interviews of Fuhrman at his racist and sexist worst. AP correspondent Linda Deutsch later recalled the moment:

> O.J. Simpson's jurors heard for the first time Tuesday Detective Mark Fuhrman uttering in his own words a racist slur, and heard testimony that the star prosecution witness advocated killing blacks.
>
> Members of the jury, which includes nine blacks, appeared shaken as the word Fuhrman denied using during the past 10 years resounded on a scratchy tape.
>
> In a stunning climax to a battle over the tapes, Simpson's lawyers persuaded the judge to change an earlier ruling and allow the jury to hear a passage in which Fuhrman spoke of women police officers.

"They don't do anything. They don't go out there and initiate contact with some six-foot-five nigger that's been in prison for seven years pumping weights," the voice on the tape said.

"Was that his [Fuhrman's] voice?" defense attorney Johnnie Cochran Jr. asked screenwriter Laura Hart McKinny.

"Yes," she said.

Jurors also were read a transcript of Fuhrman saying, "We have no niggers where I grew up."

McKinny suggested to jurors that Fuhrman's 40 other times he used the word were even worse.

The tapes demonstrated conclusively that Fuhrman was a liar and a racist, and—with the possible exception of the bloody gloves not fitting—probably did more than anything else to undermine the prosecution's case against O.J. Simpson.

Late-Trial Drama

Outside the presence of the jury, defense attorney Gerald Uelman accused Fuhrman of committing perjury on at least five occasions and asked Judge Ito for permission to confront Fuhrman about his taped statements. Uelman added, "I don't think we have plumbed the depths of the hatefulness and spite of Mark Fuhrman."

In response, Marcia Clark complained angrily to the judge that the defense was being allowed to "spread enough venom in the courtroom to sink a battleship." She acknowledged that jurors would thereafter "view Mr. Fuhrman as a racist." More important, she feared that the jurors might be enough inflamed by Fuhrman's racism as to prevent their objective judgment about the defense's claim that he planted the bloody glove at Rockingham. She called on Judge Ito to deny Uelman's request. "It's enough, your honor," Clark implored. "It's enough."

Mark Fuhrman resolved the issue the next day.

REFUTING THE EVIDENCE

In *Reasonable Doubts*, defense attorney Alan Dershowitz refuted ten key evidentiary elements upon which the prosecution built its case:

1. The police contaminated the crime scene by covering the bodies with a blanket from Nicole Brown's home, casting doubt on all the hair and fiber evidence they claimed to have recovered later.

2. The bodies of the victims were dragged around the crime scene before hair and fiber samples were taken from their clothing.

3. The police failed to notify the coroner's office in a timely fashion, as required by Los Angeles Police Department procedure.

4. The police failed to obtain a warrant to enter the Simpson estate, and instead came up with a story that seemed open to doubt.

5. The police misstated the facts on the search warrant, causing the judge eventually to find that Detective Philip Vannatter was "at least reckless" in regard to the truth.

6. The coroner's office had the autopsy performed by Dr. Irwin L. Golden, whom the prosecution eventually decided not to call as a trial witness.

7. The LAPD sent to the crime scene a trainee, Andrea Mazzola, who collected blood samples along with Dennis Fung. Mazzola had never before had primary responsibility for collecting blood evidence from a crime scene.

8. Detective Vannatter carried around O.J. Simpson's blood in a vial in an unsealed envelope for three hours and went for coffee before booking it. Trial evidence would allow the defense to argue that 1.5 cc's of blood could not be accounted for by the prosecution.

9. The criminologists failed to find blood on the back gates and socks (if blood was, in fact, there) during the original investigation and only found it several weeks after Simpson's blood sample had been taken and carried around by Vannatter.

10. The criminalists did not count the blood samples when they collected them, did not count them when put in tubes for drying, and did not count them when they were taken out of the tubes. No documented booking of samples occurred until June 16.

On September 6, outside the jury's presence, he invoked his Fifth Amendment protections against self-incrimination when asked by the defense whether he planted evidence against Simpson.

Also that day the defense ended months of speculation by announcing that O.J. Simpson would not take the stand in his own behalf. They asserted that Simpson's testimony would only extend an already overly long trial and was not necessary to answer a prosecution case already "in shambles."

Examinations and cross-examinations of several more witnesses continued for two more weeks, but the trial moved swiftly then toward its conclusion. On September 22, Judge Ito asked Simpson to state for the record that he waived his constitutional right to testify in his own defense. Out of the presence of the jury—but not the lens of television cameras—Simpson rose in court and addressed his reply to the world at large: "I did not, could not and would not have committed these crimes." He went on to say, "I have four kids. Two kids I haven't seen for a year. They ask me every week, 'Dad, how much longer?' I want this trial over."

Simpson declined to testify in his own defense during his murder trial.

Judge Ito interrupted. "Mr. Simpson," he said. "You do understand your right to testify as a witness and you choose to rest your case at this time?" Simpson nodded yes.

"In the front row," wrote AP reporter Linda Deutsch, "Simpson's grown daughter, Arnelle, sobbed." Deutsch continued:

> Across the room, victim Ronald Goldman's father clenched his hands into fists and muttered, "Murderer. Murderer.". . . Goldman's father was seething when he left the courtroom.

> "If he had a statement to make he should have gotten on the damn stand and said something and not been a coward and been unable to have the prosecution question him," Goldman said, his voice quavering. Then, referring to Simpson's statement about missing his children, he said, "I will never see my son again."

After the jurors had listened to testimony from seventy-two prosecution witnesses and fifty-four defense witnesses since testimony began on January 31, the defense and prosecution rested. The jurors did not hear Simpson's dramatic, late-trial disclaimer. Instead, in all likelihood, they heard the lingering echoes of the Fuhrman tapes rasping dissonantly in their ears.

Chapter 6

"If It Doesn't Fit, You Must Acquit"

AFTER THE DEFENSE AND PROSECUTION rested on September 22, 1995, Judge Lance Ito turned to the jury. He assured them, wrote Robert Shapiro,

> that after they heard his instructions, the prosecution and defense closing arguments would proceed as quickly as possible, without any breaks. There were scattered smiles among them, exhaustion mixed with anticipation, as though they had been on a long ocean voyage that was coming to an end.

At last, their prolonged separation from home and family, friends, jobs, coworkers, and individual lifestyles was finally drawing to a close. (The jurors were sequestered—confined to their quarters at the Hotel Inter-Continental in Los Angeles—for 267 days.)

Judge Ito Instructs the Jury

"Looking very stern, Judge Ito addressed the jury," wrote Shapiro. He then recounted the judge's instructions:

> It is now my duty to instruct you on the law as it applies to this case. . . . You must accept and follow the law as I state it to you, whether or not you agree with the law. You must not be influenced by pity for the defendant or prejudice against him. You must not be influenced by sentiment, sympathy, conjecture, passion, prejudice, public opinion,

or public feeling. You must weigh the evidence, apply the law, and reach a just verdict regardless of consequence.

Shapiro went on to convey his impressions of the jurors as they listened to the judge, briefly paraphrased as follows:

> The jury was tired. Juror number one, our odds-on favorite for foreman, was the only one taking notes. When Ito read the instruction that the defendant had no obligation to prove who committed these crimes, she carefully wrote it down.
>
> Number two was clearly exhausted. Number three, expressionless. Number four looked sleepy, while number five had looked exhausted for weeks.
>
> Juror number six looked stoic, ready to decide. Number seven seemed angry, as though she had no interest in the closing statements. "Why are they doing this?" her expression said. "I'm ready to deliberate *now*."
>
> Juror number eight was very focused, the least weary. Number nine, routinely showed the most expression; often wore her heart on her sleeve. Number ten sat ramrod straight, looking directly at Ito.
>
> Number eleven was least expressive, most anonymous; rarely showed any stress. Number twelve looked resigned, somehow pragmatic, as though thinking, "Life goes on. Let's get on with it."

As Shapiro viewed the courtroom, O.J. Simpson fingered the family Bible on the table in front of him. Arnelle Simpson wept quietly behind him. Fred Goldman and his wife sat holding hands tightly and praying silently. Their daughter Kim looked ready to cry at any moment.

Shapiro's eyes met Goldman's. "He looked back with pure hatred," Shapiro wrote. "And I understood it. I wanted to reach out to him, to tell him I was sorry. I knew I would never, never be able to do that."

Marcia's Plea

Closing arguments commenced on September 26. Co-lead prosecutor Marcia Clark stood before the jury in an ivory-colored, collarless dress, with sleeves drawn up and wrinkled at the elbows of her thin arms. "She greeted the jury, and in a voice both patient and persistent," recalled Christopher Darden, "began to methodically lay out the evidence.

"But first, there was some unfinished business. Mark Fuhrman." Darden then highlighted Marcia's plea to the jury:

> Did he lie when he testified in this courtroom . . . that he did not use racial epithets in the last ten years? Yes. Is he a racist? Yes. Is he the worst the LAPD has to offer? Yes. Do we wish this person was never hired by the LAPD? Yes.
>
> But the fact that Mark Fuhrman is a racist and lied about it on the witness stand does not mean that we haven't proven the defendant guilty beyond a reasonable doubt, and it would be a tragedy if . . . you found the defendant not guilty . . . because of the racist attitudes of one police officer.

Clark then proceeded to detail the crime scene and the testimony of limousine driver Allan Park and of houseguest Kato Kaelin and his three mysterious thumps. Darden recounted her words:

> Just think about that. Regardless of where or how they happened, just the fact that they happened shortly after the murders . . . and just before the defendant walked up his driveway in dark clothing like the dark blue or black sweat outfit that Kato described, you just put those two facts together and you realize what has happened. The defendant has come back from Bundy in a hurry.
>
> He was moving quickly down a dark, narrow pathway overhung with trees, strewn with leaves, and in his haste, he ran right into that air conditioner that was hanging over the south pathway.

Prosecutor Marcia Clark points to an evidence chart during her closing arguments. Much of the prosecution's closing remarks pleaded with the jury to pay attention to the evidence of Simpson's past violence toward Nicole.

You don't need science to tell you that. You just need reason and logic.

Clark moved on, Darden continued, to talk "about the gloves and Simpson's weird demeanor when he tried them on in the courtroom":

If I were asked to try on the gloves that were worn by the murderer of the [mother] of my children, I would not be laughing. I would not be mugging [playing to the jury and television camera]. I would not think that was funny at all. Is that the attitude you expect . . . putting on the bloody gloves that were used to murder the mother of your children?

Clark next displayed for a final time the gruesome crime-scene photographs. "This is not the mark of a professional killer," she said. "These are not efficient murders. These are murders that are really slaughters. And in that respect, they reveal a great deal about who did them. No stranger, no Colombian drug dealer."

One last time, Clark projected the image of Ron Goldman's bloody body on the seven-foot courtroom screen. "Usually, I feel I'm the only one left to speak for the victims," she said. "But Nicole and Ron are speaking to you." The families of Nicole and Ron looked on, tears streaming down their faces.

Once more Clark reminded the jurors of the violence at the Simpsons' home six years earlier. She urged them to consider what Nicole had then told a police detective who answered her 911 call: "He's going to kill me."

While playing 911 tapes from 1989 and 1993 one more time, Clark flashed a collage of photographs on the screen to illustrate her case: Nicole's bruised face, the crime scene, the trail of blood, Simpson's white Bronco, a bloody glove, and, finally, the slashed and bloodied bodies of the victims.

Clark concluded, saying, "They told you with their blood, with their hair . . . that he did it—Orenthal Simpson." She turned and faced the table where Simpson sat expressionless.

The battered face of Nicole Simpson after a beating by Simpson. After the trial, jury members would argue that they didn't understand why the prosecution presented such evidence.

"Do the Right Thing"

Marcia Clark's colleague and co-prosecutor Christopher Darden followed her to the lectern about 7:00 that night. He began his part of the prosecution's closing arguments by pointing at O.J. Simpson and saying, "I'm not afraid to point to him."

Still pointing at Simpson, he turned slowly to the jury and said, "Nobody pointed him out and said, 'He did it.' I'll point to him. Why not? The evidence all points to him. Because, when you look at the bloody ruthlessness of these murders . . . you see . . . that these killings were rage killings. Rage."

Darden, as he later wrote, went on to tell the jury:

> You have to say to yourself, well, who in the past has ever raised a hand to this woman? And who in the days and the hours leading to her death was upset with her?
>
> The killing was personal. . . . The way it was done, this was personal.

He told the trial-weary jury that things did not go well for O.J. Simpson on June 12, 1994, the day of the murders. Nicole's snub of Simpson that afternoon at his daughter Sydney's dance recital and her refusal to invite him to a family dinner at the Mezzaluna restaurant afterward may have pushed him over the edge. Darden said:

> The relationship between this man and Nicole, you know, it is like a time bomb ticking away. Just a matter of time. Just a matter of time before something really bad happened. . . . There are people with short fuses. You know, they just go off. . . . This thing was like a fuse, a bomb with a long fuse.

Darden conjectured that Simpson's girlfriend, Paula Barbieri, angered him further by severing their relationship and departing for Las Vegas without telling him. Spurned by two women he cared for deeply in the same day, Darden continued, Simpson then worked himself into a rage and prepared a plan to vent his anger and frustration on Nicole. Then, as Darden was to write later:

The next thing you know, he is in that Bronco. He is in the Bronco at 10 o'clock. . . . He is panicked and he is out of control and he needs someone or something to help calm him. And so what does he do? He calls Paula. [But] Paula is gone. Nicole is gone, and whose fault is all of this?. . . It isn't the defendant's fault; it's Nicole's fault.

We know what kind of killing this is. This is a rage killing. He's using a knife because he's there to settle a personal score, a personal vendetta. He stabs this woman in the neck and he's right there, it's one on one and the rage that he has, the anger, the hate, he has for her that night, at that time, it flows out of him . . . into the knife and into her. And he kills Ron Goldman in this rage. . . . With each thrust of that knife into her body and into Ron's body, there is a release . . . a gradual release of that anger and that rage. And he stabs, and he cuts, and he slices until that rage is gone and these people are dead.

Finally, when Simpson's murderous frenzy faded into calm relief, Darden continued, he walked—not ran or jogged—away from the crime scene, as indicated by the space between the bloody shoe prints he left behind. "He is a murderer," Darden said. "He was one hell of a good football player, but he is a murderer."

Darden completed his closing argument the next morning. "And so we've come full circle," he said. He noted later that he then "pulled out two photographs of Ron and Nicole, and the pictures froze me for a moment and I found myself talking to the pictures instead of the jury." Darden solemnly told the jury:

Ron, he was just at the wrong place at the wrong time. Nicole, she was in the wrong place for a long time.

We began with them, two very much alive and vibrant human beings. . . . We've come full circle. The only common element in all of this, the only direction in which all this points is to O.J. Simpson.

O.J. Simpson with attorneys during closing arguments. Cochran's closing arguments proposed several reasons to disbelieve the prosecution's evidence against Simpson.

After offering a brief rebuttal to the defense case, Darden ended with an appeal to the jury to "weigh the evidence . . . and do the right thing."

"Keep Your Eye on the Prize"

Johnnie Cochran Jr. took over the lectern from Darden on September 27 and opened closing arguments for the defense. Like a down-home country minister, he preached a fiery theme of racism and police misconduct. "For our side," Robert Shapiro wrote later, "Cochran began his close by taking direct aim at the L.A.P.D., calling it 'an infected investigation by a corrupt detective and a bumbling cesspool of a lab.'" Reprising Cochran's argument, Shapiro wrote:

> He challenged the mountain of evidence, especially the so-called blood trail. "If he had bloody clothes, bloody gloves, bloody shoes, then where's the blood on the doorknob? On the carpet?" Yet Cochran also lapsed into phony histrionics. He put on the knit cap, asking, "Who

am I? I'm Johnnie Cochran, with a cap on. If it doesn't
fit, you must acquit." [Cochran's implication was that
Simpson would have been recognized with or without
the knit cap, thus discrediting the prosecution theory
that Simpson wore the cap to disguise himself.]

"He said my name so many times," wrote Christopher Darden,
"I wondered for a moment if I were the one on trial." Darden
went on to write:

> Cochran showed a photograph of Simpson with his children
> and asked snidely, "Where is the fuse now, Mr. Darden?"
>
> He said that our case was slipping away as soon as I had
> Simpson try on the gloves.
>
> "You'll always remember those gloves, when Darden
> asked him to try it [sic] on, didn't fit. . . . No matter what
> they do, they can't make them fit." He said prosecutors
> would "do anything to contort, distort the facts." He
> repeated his themes, "If it doesn't fit, you must acquit,"
> and "journey to justice."

"The next morning [September 28], Cochran came back to continue his close," Robert Shapiro wrote, concluding his short
summation of Cochran's oration this way:

> At first, he talked from his heart, he talked from his soul,
> he talked from the Bible. It was almost as if he was
> preaching. His rhythm would get going, and you almost
> expected the jury to fall into a call-and-response pattern.
> "If you're untruthful in small things, you cannot be
> believed in large things," he said. . . .
>
> And then he made a terrible mistake. He linked Fuhr-
> man, a banal, petty, mindless racist, with the most mon-
> strous murderer of all time, Adolph [sic] Hitler. In less
> than a minute, he accelerated from a corrupt Los Ange-
> les cop to the Holocaust itself, suggesting to this jury
> that they could stop Fuhrman, as the Germans had not

stopped Hitler. "Maybe this is why you're sitting here, the right people, at the right time," he said. It was gratuitous, inflammatory, and just plain wrong. Worse, as far as this case was concerned, it was completely unnecessary.

Using biblical phrasing, Cochran called Mark Fuhrman and Philip Vannatter "twin devils of deception." "I couldn't believe they were painting Vannatter with the same brush they used on Fuhrman," wrote Christopher Darden.

Cochran renounced racism and police corruption again and again, urging the jurors to "Stop this cover-up! Stop this cover-up! You are the consciences of this community." Then, noted Alan Dershowitz, Cochran said:

> Both prosecutors have now agreed that . . . there's a lying, perjuring, genocidal racist and he's testified willfully false in this case on a number of scores. . . . You are empowered to say we're not going to take that anymore. . . . [W]hen a witness lies in a material part of his testimony, you can wipe out all of his testimony as a judge of the facts. . . . You're the ones who send a message.

In words reminiscent of the civil rights movement, Cochran said, "I know you will stay the course, keep your eye on the prize, and do the right thing."

Reasonable Doubt

DNA expert Barry Scheck continued the defense's arguments with a more detached, scientific analysis of the evidence. "Barry Scheck took on the real work," Christopher Darden noted later, "arguing the merits of their case, which he did strongly and effectively." Robert Shapiro agreed:

> Barry Scheck's portion of the closing statement went a long way toward restoring my faith. "Ladies and gentlemen, as you've heard, my partner Peter Neufeld and I are from New York. More specifically, we're from Brooklyn," he began, and then proceeded, point by point, to rebut the prosecution's forensics evidence.

DEALING THE RACE CARD

Few would argue that race did not play a major role in the Simpson trial, but many observers continued to view the case in simpler terms, unfettered by racial implications. For instance, in *The O.J. Simpson Trial in Black and White*, journalist Tom Elias wrote:

> I continued to see the case as plain and simple murder. Yes, I believed, it was possible for the police to lie and for some cops to be racist, and for Simpson still to be guilty. But such distinctions were not part of Cochran's final statement to the jury, one that struck me as pure demagoguery [an appeal to prejudices]. Especially offensive to me as the son of Holocaust survivors was his comparison of Fuhrman to Adolf Hitler. Even if everything Fuhrman claimed he did on the McKinny tapes were true, he never approached being a Hitler. Cochran's defense of his remark was that Fuhrman's acts were like those of a fascist. But Hitler had followers and sought to take over first a nation and then the world. Fuhrman had no followers, never aspired to be a leader and wanted only a pension, so he could move away from the ethnics he so scorned. So as the [Jewish] Anti-Defamation League said immediately on hearing Cochran's speech, his Hitler metaphor trivialized a profound historical tragedy.

Using Dr. Lee's example of cockroaches in a bowl of spaghetti, he pointed to Nicole's blood [allegedly] planted on O.J.'s socks, and O.J.'s blood showing up after the murders on the rear gate at Nicole's condominium. "How many cockroaches do you need?" he asked.

"Every explanation that they're desperately trying to come up with is a highly improbable influence," Scheck said. "The most likely and probable explanation is the one that is not for the timid or the faint at heart: *Somebody played with this evidence!*". . .

"That's a reasonable doubt for this case," Scheck continued. "Period. End of sentence. End of case."

Johnnie Cochran returned to finish. He explained reasonable doubt to the jury and warned, "You can't trust their [the prosecution's] message. . . . If it doesn't fit, you must acquit."

Defense attorney Barry Scheck points to a chart depicting the LAPD as a "black hole" during closing arguments. The defense claimed that the evidence was so corrupted that no conclusions about Simpson's guilt could be made.

The Verdict

After a brief rebuttal by the prosecution, the trial of O.J. Simpson ended. The jurors, who had sat in rapt attention throughout the closing arguments, then faced the considerable task of sifting through fifty thousand pages of court transcripts and weighing 437 pieces of evidence. Crowds were already gathering outside the courtroom.

In his final instructions to the jury, Judge Lance A. Ito directed them to disregard lawyer warnings that "the world is watching," reminding them that their duty is to "reach a just verdict regardless of the consequences." He emphasized, "You are not partisans or advocates, but impartial judges of the facts."

The jury of nine blacks, two whites, and one Hispanic filed out of the courtroom and returned to their hotel for one last weekend. Jury deliberations commenced on Monday, October 2.

Considering the nature and complexity of the trial and the mass of documents and physical evidence confronting the jurors, most expert legal observers expected a long deliberation—anywhere from a week to more than a month. To the surprise of the entire world, the jury reached a verdict in under four hours.

On the morning of October 3, 1995, Deirdre Robertson, the judge's clerk read their verdict, the same for both counts of murder charged against the defendant: "We, the jury . . . find the defendant, Orenthal James Simpson, not guilty. . . ."

"Jaws dropped," wrote AP correspondent Linda Deutsch. "There were gasps in the courtroom. Simpson appeared stunned, as did his attorney, Carl Douglas, a second-stringer on the legal team assigned the mundane task of sitting next to Simpson during testimony readbacks."

"Instantly, it seemed as though the whole room behind me was in tears," Robert Shapiro recalled, "the Goldmans and Browns in grief and anger, the Simpsons in relief and gratitude." Shapiro, in a brief assessment of the verdict, wrote:

Simpson clenches his fists in victory after the jury's verdict of not guilty. Simpson's acquittal shocked people throughout the nation.

The Goldman family reacts after the jury verdict. Believing that a great injustice was done, the family brought a wrongful death suit against Simpson.

> I felt, and still feel, that the jury had reached the right conclusion in this case. It was a victory, a legal victory, and [Simpson's] people could certainly congratulate each other for the long months of hard work and effort that had produced the result we'd hoped for. Nevertheless, two people were still dead. It wasn't time for a celebration. It wasn't New Year's Eve.

Christopher Darden viewed the verdict through a glass darkly:

> Afterward, I was numb . . . trying to imagine how they could come to a reasoned decision in just four hours. It was impossible. They owed it to the people of California to weigh the evidence and reassess the testimony and they hadn't. . . . Instead, they did just what Johnnie Cochran asked them to do. . . . They sent a message.

When questioned by the media later about how the jury came to its decision, juror Brenda Moran said that the prosecution failed in a number of areas to prove its case beyond a reasonable doubt. As an example, she cited the gloves. "In plain English," she said, "the gloves didn't fit."

Afterword

"Nothing Shocks Me Anymore"

AND SO IT ENDED. "On Tuesday, October 3—after a previous
day's deliberation of an astonishingly brief four and a half
hours [*sic*]—the jury found O.J. Simpson not guilty of the murders of Nicole Brown Simpson and Ronald Goldman," wrote
Sheila Weller, author and Ms. Simpson's biographer. "The
brevity of the deliberations seems to indicate that the jurors vir-
tually dismissed, wholesale, the prosecution case."

The verdict rocked the nation like a California earthquake
and left America's white and black communities split with a gap-
ing fissure. Not since the civil rights movement of the 1960s had
the racial divide in this country shown itself so clearly as it did in
the public's reaction to the Simpson verdict.

Battle Lines

"In New York's Times Square, as the verdict reading was shown
on the giant Sony Jumbotron TV, black spectators erupted in
cheers and honked their car horns," wrote AP correspondent
Michael Fleeman. "Most whites remained subdued." Fleeman
continued:

> At Howard University, a class of black law students
> cheered. At the University of Utah College of Law, 85
> percent of one mostly white class said he was guilty. And
> one picture in *Newsweek* captured it all: a group of stu-
> dents at Augustana College in Rock Island, Illinois, the

black students applauding and leaping in joy, the white students frozen in stunned silence.

A black-majority jury of 10 women and two men reached a verdict after deliberating less than four hours. A nation that couldn't talk about the Simpson case enough struggled to understand why the jury hardly wanted to talk about it at all.

The verdict was not guilty on all counts in the murders of Ronald Goldman and Nicole Brown Simpson. To some people, that just didn't seem right; it seemed to them like a murderer buying an acquittal the way he bought his Ferrari, aided and abetted by a high-paid team of con men that duped a jury with a high-stakes form of three-card monte. To others, it was sweet justice, a long-overdue nationally televised example of the system finally doing for a black man reared in the projects what it's done for decades for white men raised in the suburbs. The battle lines were drawn, whites on one side, blacks on the other.

Given the obvious racial division in the United States, the first assumption of most who followed the televised saga of O.J. Simpson was that the verdict grew out of the racial biases of a mostly black jury. But jurors denied that race influenced their verdict.

Race No Influence

The Simpson jury collectively asserted that their verdict derived solely from the prosecution's inability to prove its case beyond a reasonable doubt. Armanda Cooley, the jury foreperson, answered critics of the jury's decision in clear, resonant terms, writing:

It's important that people know this was not a racist thing. I'm black and Mr. Simpson is black. However, Mr. Simpson lives in a white world. When we signed up to do our civic duty, it was People versus Orenthal J. Simpson, not People versus Racism or People versus the Politicians or People versus Battered Women and Children. I'm just as sensitive to racism as the next person is, but people need

Students at Augustana College in Rock Island, Illinois, react in a typical way as the Simpson verdict is read—blacks joyously proclaim victory while white students express shock and dismay.

to know that was not our cause whatsoever. I don't care what color Mr. Simpson is. If the evidence had been there to find him guilty, then that's what I would have done.

Yet poll upon poll taken in the aftermath of the Simpson verdict showed that nearly 75 percent of white Americans polled believed that Simpson was guilty, and that the black-majority jury acquitted him as a payback for past white injustices to blacks.

Understanding Evidence

But what of the many criticisms that, as a group, the jury was not intellectually up to the task of understanding and evaluating the wealth of complex scientific evidence offered by the prosecution? Journalist Tom Elias, for instance, wrote that the jury selection process eliminated any prospective juror "with significant respect for science or scientific evidence." He further noted:

This was clearly reflected in the jurors' behavior once the trial began. Day after day, several appeared to have difficulty staying awake, especially during the prosecution's almost two-month-long presentation of the DNA blood evidence. Others seemed almost never to pay attention to any of the voluminous scientific evidence presented by prosecutors.

Jury foreperson Cooley responded to such criticism this way:

> No matter what anybody thinks, we paid close attention throughout the trial. We all had extensive notes and were all thinking along the same lines when it came down to deliberation. Still, I think boredom became a factor during some of the testimony from the expert witnesses. When they tried so hard to explain things to you, it almost seemed like they thought they were dealing with a bunch of illiterate, ignorant people. After a while, when you're hearing something repeated over and over, you probably do get a bored look. Even Judge Ito would be yawning and going off the deep end sometimes. Especially when it came down to the DNA experts. . . . But we had no problem with their presentation. We all understood. . . . A lot of us felt we could now earn a medical degree.

Although the prosecution demonstrated O.J. Simpson's history of spousal abuse beyond question—crucial to establishing him as a violent person capable of committing murder—it seemed to miss the mark with jurors. Two days after the trial, juror Brenda Moran told reporters that she and her fellow jurors paid no attention to Simpson's long record of domestic violence. "This was a murder trial, not domestic abuse," she smirked. "If you want to get tried for domestic abuse, go in another courtroom and get tried for that."

Sequestration

Many observers felt that jury sequestration might have influenced the jurors to rush to a verdict in their ardor to end their long confinement. As a case in point, Tom Elias recalled that a former juror who had been sequestered for seven months on the Charles Manson trial in 1971, had told him, "I would have done anything to end it." Elias then recounted the tale of a Simpson juror:

When the Simpson jury finally began deliberating, its first vote was 10-2 in favor of acquittal. Anise Aschenbach, a 60-year-old divorcee and retired gas company employee, was one of the two who initially wanted to convict. On her questionnaire, she said that while serving on an earlier jury, she had been the only one wishing to convict on the first vote. But she held out and by the time a verdict was rendered, she recalled, she had turned her colleagues around.

Aschenbach made no such heroic effort this time. After many months of sequestration, she was apparently too tired, or too despairing, to convince anyone of her point of view. And she didn't want to be a part of a hung jury. "I thought of all the months, all the money, this case not being resolved . . . ," she mused later. She also said, "I think he probably did it and that's the pits. . . . Chances are good he did it, and that's a shame." But she switched

Simpson juror Brenda Moran defends the jury's verdict of not guilty. Many could not believe the short amount of time it took for the jury to reach a verdict.

her vote and Simpson walked away a free man. "It doesn't make me feel very good," she said later. "But on the other hand, [Simpson is] not a serial killer." There's a rationalization sure to promote respect for the jury system!

Four Points to Ponder

In fairness, it should be noted that prosecutors refuted, item for item, each of the seven items proposed by Professor Dershowitz as likely to have influenced the jury's decision. Moreover, as to the possibility that the police conspired to plant and corrupt evidence in order to frame O.J. Simpson, at least four things should be considered in the interest of truth: (1) a police conspiracy would require the participation of upward of fifteen police personnel, most of whom did not know one another before the murders; (2) upon discovery, a conspirator would risk immediate termination of employment and possibly become subject to prosecution under California law for a felony punishable by death; (3) at least a dozen officers were at the Bundy crime scene before Detective Fuhrman's arrival to establish that there was no second glove at the scene; and (4) blood evidence discovered early in the investigation—on the bloody glove and at Bundy and Rockingham—could not have been planted by police using a portion of Simpson's blood draw, since that blood did not become available until Simpson's return from Chicago several hours later. The utter unlikelihood of a police conspiracy apparently did not influence the jurors.

After reviewing the timeline testimony of limo driver Allan Park, the jury took a second poll and voted unanimously to acquit. "We never did know who the other guilty vote was, and still don't," Armanda Cooley wrote, then addressed the question of the jury's short deliberation:

> There has been a lot of criticism about how long—or short—the deliberation was. I say, where is it written how long the deliberation should be? Number one, we were in lockup for eight or nine months. . . . [W]hen you're in that room by yourself at night, you're deliberating with yourself. . . . So it did not take another nine months in that [jury] room to deliberate the case, because everybody was going through the same thing. . . .

We walked into that room and discovered that everybody was in tune to the same thing. That's the reason why it didn't take a long time. The law states that all you need is one reasonable doubt. We had several reasonable doubts. . . . We went through all the exhibits and the evidence. We did all that before we reached a verdict.

It is worth repeating that there were 437 pieces of evidence and a trial transcript numbering fifty thousand pages.

Cameras in the Courtroom

Another topic that came under the guns of fast-shooting critics was the question of television cameras in the courtroom. Many felt that the cameras' presence in court materially changed the conduct of the proceedings in that trial participants continually played to the camera.

Critics claimed that two trials were being conducted simultaneously—one for the jury and one for the public. Under the eye of the camera, they said, lawyers, and even the judge, felt undue pressures to perform for a vast TV audience. This resulted in disrupting and distorting the judiciary process as it would normally be practiced.

Other pundits hailed the use of cameras in the courtroom as a New Age civics lesson brought to millions of viewers through the magic of modern technology. The jury, as it were, is still out on this one.

Police and the System

Nor did the police and the system escape the Simpson saga without incurring the wrath of cynics—from press and pundits, from far and near. "The police DNA lab may not be quite the 'cesspool of contamination' the defense suggested," wrote Michael Fleeman for the Associated Press, "but it certainly has quality-control problems." Fleeman explained:

At best, police technicians were sloppy. At best, detectives cut corners and stretched the truth. So much could have been avoided if police just followed their own rules. If Detective Philip Vannatter had just booked the vial of Simpson's blood into evidence the way he was supposed to, rather than taking it back to Simpson's house where key blood evidence was found, the defense would have lost an entire line of cross-examination—and the jury would have had one less reason to acquit.

In the aftermath of the Simpson case, people were reexamining the jury system, the way jurors are selected, the extent to which juries represent the population, the manner in which juries consider evidence, and the issue of whether unanimous verdicts are necessary in criminal cases. Some even were saying the jury system was broken and that judges alone should hear the evidence. But in the racially-charged Simpson aftermath, simply suggesting reforms to the jury system created more controversy, as blacks accused reform-promoting whites of whining over a verdict that didn't come out the way whites thought it should.

The American justice system will continue to evolve in its search for truth. But no one suggests that its evolution will be easy.

The Way of Justice?

Neither will O.J. Simpson find it easy to resume life as he once knew it. In the immediate future, he faces civil suits [ongoing as of this publication] for wrongful death suits filed by both the Goldmans and the Browns. "The Goldmans," wrote Michael Fleeman, "have vowed to sue Simpson out of every Hertz dollar he ever made; it was their only remaining weapon." This alone effectively puts Simpson's life on hold for the time being. Perhaps Armanda Cooley had it right when she wrote:

O.J. Simpson may be acquitted, but the public and the media will never quit. O.J. will never rest easy again. Wherever he goes, he will never be the O.J. that he was before. What he gets, he will have to work to get it. Before, it was easy. You could mingle and run around. But I do believe it will never be as easy as it was before

A free man, Simpson enjoys a game of golf. Many still find it hard to believe that justice was done.

for him—that's all in the past.

Some might say that Justice, like God, works in mysterious ways.

Light and Shadows

The case files of both the Los Angeles District Attorney's office and the Los Angeles Police Department have been closed in the absence of any evidence whatsoever pointing to any suspect other than O.J. Simpson in the double-homicide of Nicole Brown Simpson and Ronald Lyle Goldman.

Shortly after his acquittal, Simpson publicly declared that he would dedicate himself for the rest of his life to finding the "real" murderer or murderers of his former wife and her friend. So far, there has been little indication of such an effort on his part and no reported results therefrom.

In May 1996, Simpson, in an apparent attempt to begin reestablishing public acceptance, appeared before a debating group at Oxford in England. Of that appearance, Barry Hillenbrand, in an article for *Time* magazine, wrote:

> After receiving a warm round of applause from the 1,000 students crammed together on the brown leather benches of the elegant 1871 Union Debating Chamber, Simpson tried a few quips, only to be interrupted by Fiona Maazel, an American at Oxford for her junior year abroad. "You can make your jokes, but this isn't funny," she said. "Your wife was murdered. Your history of assault and abuse

makes this an insult." The audience was stunned and embarrassed. Maazel was escorted out of the hall.

Good humor and grace under fire count for a lot in Oxford debates, and Maazel's attack helped Simpson win over the crowd. He stayed cool.

Today, O.J. Simpson walks free—acquitted of a heinous crime by a jury of his peers. Whether he walks in the pure light of innocence or in the shadow of damnation, only O.J. knows.

In the end the jury favored the arguments of the black preacher-lawyer Cochran over those of the black prosecutor Darden. When asked if he believed the quick verdict, a benumbed, incredulous Christopher Darden could only say, "I think I have to believe it. It's happening. Nothing shocks me anymore."

Glossary

acquittal: A setting free from the charge of an offense by verdict, sentence, or other legal process.

appellate court: A court having the power to review and overturn the decisions of another tribunal.

arraignment: A court hearing in which a defendant answers charges of a crime brought against him or her.

autopsy: An examination after death to determine its cause.

criminalist: One who collects, catalogs, analyzes, and preserves evidence.

cross-examination: A secondary interrogation of a witness in an attempt to discredit the answers to previous questions.

direct examination: An initial interrogation of a witness.

DNA: Deoxyribonucleic acid, often described as the "building block" or "genetic fingerprint" of human beings.

forensics: A science that deals with the relation and application of medical facts to legal problems.

pathologist: One who interprets and diagnoses the changes caused by disease in tissues and body fluids.

perjury: A voluntary violation of an oath or vow either by swearing to what is untrue or by omission to do what has been promised under oath.

sequestration: The act of isolating a jury from exterior influences.

serology: A science dealing with serums, especially their reactions and properties.

subpeona: A writ commanding a person designated in it to appear in court under a penalty for failure to do so.

voir dire: A preliminary examination to determine the competence of a witness or juror.

Timeline

1994

June 12: Nicole Brown Simpson and friend Ronald Goldman viciously slain in front of Nicole's Bundy condo.

June 17: O.J. Simpson charged with two counts of murder.

July 22: O.J. pleads "absolutely, 100 percent not guilty" to the charges against him.

1995

January 11: Jury sequestered.

January 24: Trial begins.

March 21: Houseguest Brian "Kato" Kaelin testifies about O.J.'s demeanor and whereabouts on the night of the murders.

March 29: Limousine driver Allan Park recounts time sequence on the night of June 12.

May 10: Dr. Robin Cotton begins DNA testimony.

June 15: O.J. Simpson tries on bloody gloves; they don't fit.

July 6: The prosecution ends.

July 10: The defense begins.

August 10: Forensic pathologist Dr. Michael Baden refutes the prosecution's forensic evidence and single-killer theory.

August 21: Dr. Henry Lee testifies that "something wrong" with the prosecution evidence.

September 5: The jury hears two excerpts from Fuhrman tapes.

September 6: Mark Fuhrman, with the jury absent, retakes the stand and invokes his Fifth Amendment privilege.

September 7: The defense announces that O.J. Simpson will not testify in his own behalf.

September 22: Both sides rest their cases.

September 26–28: Closing arguments.

September 29: The case goes to the jury.

October 2: The jury reaches a verdict in less than four hours.

For Further Reading

Tracy Kennedy and Judith Kennedy with Alan Abrahamson, *Mistrial of the Century: A Private Diary of the Jury System on Trial*. Beverly Hills, CA: Dove Books, 1995. Tracy Kennedy—a juror on the O.J. Simpson trial until dismissed by Judge Lance A. Ito on March 17, 1995—and his wife describe what happened during the trial and sequestration.

Michael Knox with Mike Walker, *The Private Diary of an OJ Simpson Juror: Behind the Scenes of the Trial of the Century*. Beverly Hills, CA: Dove Books, 1995. The author, Juror 620 in the O.J. Simpson trial, reveals the "shocking secret" that forced him off the trial.

Frank McLynn, *Famous Trials: Cases That Made History*. Pleasantville, NY: The Reader's Digest Association, 1995. This fascinating volume offers vivid re-creations of thirty-four famous trials spanning two thousand years.

Faye D. Resnick with Jeanne V. Bell, *Shattered: In the Eye of the Storm*. Beverly Hills, CA: Dove Books, 1996. The author reflects on how the loss of her best friend, Nicole Brown Simpson, has affected her life and in so doing "opens the door to the understanding of battered women everywhere"; a candid, distressing, and very personal memoir.

Peter Roberts, *OJ: 101 Theories, Conspiracies & Alibis*. Diamond Bar, CA: Goldtree Press, 1995. Roberts poses "101 intriguing theories, conspiracies, and alibis pointing towards O.J. Simpson's guilt or innocence in the murders of his ex-wife and her friend.

Stephen Singular, *Legacy of Deception: An Investigation of Mark Fuhrman and Racism in the L.A.P.D.* Beverly Hills, CA: Dove Books, 1995. The author implies a number of sinister scenarios pertinent to the O.J. Simpson case and raises many provocative but unanswered questions.

Works Consulted

Mark Cerasini, *O.J. Simpson: American Hero, American Tragedy.* New York: Pinnacle Books, 1994. Although put together in haste, the book presents an interesting overview of Simpson's life up to the time of his arrest.

Armanda Cooley, Carrie Bess, and Marsha Rubin-Jackson, as told to Tom Byrnes, with Mike Walker, *Madam Foreman: A Rush to Judgment?* Beverly Hills, CA: Dove Books, 1995. This book is a social commentary that recaps ten months of jury sequestration.

Christopher Darden, with Jess Walter, *In Contempt.* New York: HarperCollins Publishers, 1996. Darden, with unflinching candor, details the inner workings of the prosecution during the O.J. Simpson trial.

Alan M. Dershowitz, *Reasonable Doubts: The O.J. Simpson Case and the Criminal Justice System.* New York: Simon & Schuster, 1996. "This book," writes Dershowitz, "is for the many thoughtful observers who sincerely and understandably believe that O.J. Simpson killed Nicole Brown and Ronald Goldman, and that the jury's verdict of Not Guilty was therefore a miscarriage of justice."

Linda Deutsch and Michael Fleeman, and the writers and photographers of the Associated Press, *Verdict: The Chronicle of the O.J. Simpson Trial.* Kansas City, MO: Andrews and McNeel, 1995. Deutsch and Fleeman, two veteran Associated Press reporters, collaborate on a comprehensive account of one of the most controversial legal cases of our time.

Tom Elias and Dennis Schatzman, *The O.J. Simpson Trial in Black and White.* Los Angeles: General Publishing Group, 1996. Two respected national journalists who shared seat C-12 in Judge Lance Ito's courtroom—one man black, the other white—confront the dominant theme in the O.J. Simpson trial: race.

Clifford L. Linedecker, *Marcia Clark: Her Private Trials and Public Triumphs*. New York: Pinnacle Books, 1995. The author tells the story of "a sheltered, studious young woman born into a religious Jewish family" who becomes "a hard-hitting prosecutor and national media star."

Faye D. Resnick, with Mike Walker, *Nicole Brown Simpson: The Private Diary of a Life Interrupted*. Beverly Hills, CA: Dove Books, 1994. Resnick, Nicole Brown Simpson's "best friend and sometimes roommate," describes Nicole as "a woman trapped, like far too many others, in the violent cycle of spousal abuse."

Robert L. Shapiro, with Larkin Warren, *The Search for Justice: A Defense Attorney's Brief on the O.J. Simpson Case*. New York: Warner Books, 1996. The dramatic story of how Shapiro put together the so-called Dream Team and planned the defense of O.J. Simpson against what appeared to be a mountain of incriminating evidence and impossible odds.

Sheila Weller, *Raging Heart: The Intimate Story of the Tragic Marriage of O.J. and Nicole Brown Simpson*. New York: Pocket Books, 1995. Written by an acclaimed journalist, with "the unprecedented cooperation of Nicole Brown Simpson's family," and with "exclusive access to O.J. and Nicole's friends," this book reveals the dark side of a stormy marriage destined to end in tragedy. Kim Cunningham wrote in *People* magazine that Weller's book "leaves no reasonable doubt about who committed the crime." The book includes eight pages of photographs.

Index

Picture Credits

About the Author

Earle Rice Jr. attended San Jose City College and Foothill College on the San Francisco peninsula, after serving nine years with the U.S. Marine Corps.

He has authored nineteen books for young adults, including fast-action fiction and adaptations of *Dracula*, *All Quiet on the Western Front*, and *The Grapes of Wrath*. Mr. Rice has written several books for Lucent, including *The Cuban Revolution* and seven books in the popular *Great Battles* series. He has also written articles and short stories and has previously worked for several years as a technical writer.

Mr. Rice is a former senior design engineer in the aerospace industry who now devotes full time to his writing. He lives in Julian, California, with his wife, daughter, two granddaughters, five cats, and a dog.